10.29
D

INDIAN WARS

RICHARD H. DILLON

INDIAN WARS

1850-1890

Exeter Books

NEW YORK

Half title page: The Sioux brave **Low Dog**, a veteran of the Battle of Little Big Horn, was archetypical of the enraged warrior who fought on through the late nineteenth century despite overwhelming odds.

Title page: A detail of the painting *Jumped* in which the Montana artist Charles Russell suggests how mounted Plains Indians made hit and run surprise attacks on prairie schooners out in the open grasslands.

Below: In 1870 William Henry Jackson recorded **Chief Washakie's encampment** of skin lodges or *tipis*. Always friendly toward the white man Washakie and his Shoshone braves even scouted and fought for the Army against the Sioux.

Contents

THE GOLD RUSH AND INDIAN WARS IN THE 1850s

From the time that gold was discovered in California and western expansion began in earnest to the last battle at Wounded Knee, conflicts between the Indian and the white man plagued America. No simple solution was possible, given the number and variety of Indian tribal groups, the shifting US policy toward Indians, and the gap between cultures. The history of Indian wars in North America is a violent story, and one dotted with incidents of individual glory, cunning, treachery, courage and despair. The end of the story is already well-known, but it is the struggles and battles leading up to this end that give it a lasting significance, illuminating the characters of the men who fought for their lives, their homeland and their convictions.

The period leading up to the Civil War was marked by wars in the Pacific Northwest and lesser skirmishes, often provoked by overzealous Army volunteers, as Indians were pushed into allocated territories. Installed across the frontier as a peace-keeping force, the Army had not yet geared up for major campaigns against the Indians, especially as the Civil War loomed on the horizon. At the same time, however, gold-seekers formed an increasing westward flow—clothed in the guise of Manifest Destiny—disrupting the Indians' way of life. For hundreds of miles along the banks of the Platte they stripped away the grass and firewood and collected every dried-up buffalo chip for kindling. The vast buffalo herd of the Plains was split in two, especially by the building of the transcontinental railroad. This was the most devastating effect of Western migration on the Plains Indians who bore the assault with stoic tolerance. Hostilities were usually limited to thefts of livestock for food or pilfering of property, often out of sheer curiosity. Violence was rare at first, and murder was confined almost exclusively to the Humboldt River of Nevada, where Paiutes picked off stragglers.

In 1851 Indian agent Tom Fitzpatrick joined his boss, Superintendent of Indian Affairs David D Mitchell, in a treaty-making council at Fort Laramie, Wyoming. The Arapaho chief, Little Raven, described Fitzpatrick as the one really fair agent that his people had ever known. Fitzpatrick was best known as Broken Hand because an exploding rifle had blown off several fingers. He was also called White Hair because a scare from a band of Gros Ventres was said to have bleached his hair overnight.

To Fitz's amazement, 10,000 Indians camped around the post. The entire Army, stretched from Maine to California, totaled only 10,000 men, and that was on paper. Its actual strength was probably closer to 8000.

The dominant Sioux were present in force, accompanied by their loyal allies, the Northern Cheyennes and Arapahos. The Hidatsas and Mandans came to the Big Talk, too. Enemies of the Sioux—the Crows or Absarokas, the Gros Ventres, Arikaras, even Assiniboines from far-off Canada—also dragged their *travois* to the Laramie Fork of the North Platte. The Pawnees were too hostile to the Dakotas (Lakota), or Sioux, to show up. Curiously, the Kiowas and Comanches, friends of the Sioux, chose not to come. They told friendly whites that there would be too many horse thieves, meaning both Crows and Dakotas. But the wary Shoshones made an appearance, led by their friend and protector, Jim Bridger. Jim, nicknamed Old Gabe, promised to make sure that the Sioux were peaceful.

Several times during the proceedings, inter-tribal rivalries almost boiled over into violent clashes. But they were averted by the prompt actions of the 270 troopers who policed the Big Talk.

Earlier, the US Government had promised the tribes a vast country of their own—one great reservation beyond the Missouri and the so-called Permanent Indian Frontier. But now that promise was abandoned as a result of the California Gold Rush and the growth of the Concept of Manifest Destiny, which held that it was ordained by God that the persistent westward drive of white Americans should, rightfully, fill the continent from sea to sea.

By Fitzpatrick's 'Treaty of Horse Creek', the Indians not only guaranteed travelers the right of safe passage through Indian country and permitted the building of roads and forts, but they also accepted their own allocation to specific tribal 'territories', reservation-like tracts, with boundaries as fixed as those of the states of the Union. And they promised to abstain from warring on each other. The Federal Government guaranteed that the Indians' lands would be theirs forever. Weary of debate, the chiefs x'd their signatures to the document so that Broken Hand would give out the presents that he had promised them.

Opposite page: Horse Chief was a typical Pawnee Plains warrior whom the great painter of American Indians, George Catlin (1796–1872), painted on his first trip west in 1832. Until this pivotal trip Catlin had been a New York portrait painter.

Above: Even before they acquired firearms, America's Indians made use of a varied armory of weapons of war. These included bows and arrows, the latter which were either flint or obsidian-tipped until the white man introduced steel to the redmen; buffalo-hide shields, which were hung with feathers; and lances, which were favored by the Comanches who often had to charge Mexican *lanceros* similarly armed.

Opposite page: Unable to get 'action' shots of **Paiutes** in 1872, John K (Jack) Hillers resorted to posing three braves in costume.

In 1853, at Fort Atkinson near the later site of Dodge City, Kansas, Fitzpatrick carried out a similar treaty-signing with the southern tribes that had refused to have anything to do with the Sioux at Laramie.

Broken Hand knew that intertribal warfare would continue. It was ingrained in the Indian's nature. Prowess in combat was ten times as important as skill in hunting. Indians would fight to gain territory, plunder or revenge, but most of all to gratify their lust for personal glory. And the greatest glory of all came from counting *coups* in hand-to-hand combat. He also knew that chiefs, in peace or war,

had no authority to speak as sovereigns for all of their people. This idea was a conceit of functionaries in Washington who found it convenient to treat with Indian chiefs as if they were European princes or Asian potentates.

But Fitzpatrick was not banking solely on Indian Bureau paperwork to keep the peace. He put most of his faith in the string of forts in the West, weak as they were. The Army's strength had sagged to a dangerous low after the Mexican War's end in 1848. Its effective power was reduced further by epidemics of drunkenness, disease and desertion. Most of the rank and file was composed of the greenest of soldiery. Many were Irish and German immigrant boys, down on their luck and ready to try anything after the abject squalor and grinding poverty of Eastern tenements.

Grattan's Massacre

The ink was hardly dry on the two optimistic treaties when hostilities broke out between the Army and the powerful Teton Sioux. On 18 August 1854, six months after Fitzpatrick died of pneumonia in Washington while seeking approval of his treaties, a Miniconjou Sioux, High Forehead, visited his Brulé relatives and Oglala friends. Needing some cowhide, he left the 4000 Indians camped on the North Platte to receive their annuities, and shot an arrow into a Mormon's footsore cow. Probably the owner was on the point of leaving the beast behind, but he complained to Fort Laramie's commanding officer, Second Lieutenant Hugh B Fleming. Fleming was willing to negotiate for recompense, but was hesitant about arresting or punishing Indians without an Indian agent being present.

One of Fleming's subordinates, Brevet Second Lieutenant John L Grattan, begged permission to deal with the Sioux. He was just out of West Point and had not even received his commission. But he had frequently stated that his greatest desire was to fight the Sioux.

The cocky Grattan took only 30 volunteers. He was convinced that all Sioux were cowards. As for the Cheyennes, he bragged that, with ten good men, he would beat them. With an added ten, he would thrash all of the Plains tribes! As he left the post, he postured with absurd naivete, dramatically promising to 'conquer or die.'

The brevet lieutenant drew up his small force in a battle line in the camp of Conquering Bear's Brulés in the North Platte Valley west of Ash Hollow. Through a drunken interpreter, Grattan lectured and abused the Sioux. The chief offered horses in payment for the cow, but would not deliver up the Miniconjou. The drunkard now tried to throw a scare into the Sioux. He told them that the Army was coming for them and 'would eat their hearts, raw.'

Conquering Bear tried to calm the hotheads on both sides of the quarrel, but someone opened fire. Possibly it was all an accident—a nervous private discharging his musket by mistake. But musket firing came from both sides and the cannoneers with Grattan's two menacing howitzers took the first shot as a signal. One of them dropped a round almost on top of Conquering Bear, mortally wounding the chief as he cried out to his people not to shoot.

Now the village turned into a hornets' nest, even before other Sioux rode up to join the fray. The foolish Grattan tried to fall back to the fort, but the Sioux easily cut off his retreat. The combat came to be called **Grattan's Massacre** because the Indians destroyed his command to the last man. (One soldier made it to Fort Laramie but died there

of his wounds.)

Older men prevented the angry young braves from attacking the fort, where Fleming had only 42 men. After stripping the warehouse of the annuity goods, the Tetons broke up into small bands.

The Commissioner of Indian Affairs decreed that the Army had exceeded its authority. Grattan's action was illegal; he had no right to arrest Indians for thefts. But Secretary of War Jefferson Davis called the Grattan affair part of a deliberate plan by the Sioux to loot all annuity and trade goods in their area. And he wanted to make an example of the Sioux for giving the Army such a black eye.

Revenge at Ash Hollow and Solomon River

Jeff Davis had just the man for the job of avenging Grattan. Colonel William S Harney, born in 1800, was a steel-hard soldier still, tempered by Seminole and Mexican War service. The fiery-tongued, profane six-footer was said to have hated all Indians with a passion ever since he had been obliged to run ignominiously for cover—and for his life—in his underwear during the Second Florida War. Cowering in palmetto and sawgrass, scratching mosquito welts, he had had plenty of time to work up a lasting hatred for all redskins, not just Seminoles.

Harney led 600 infantry, cavalry and artillery out of Fort Kearny, Nebraska to **Ash Hollow**, on 24 August 1855. For some reason, fatalism perhaps, Conquering Bear's successor, Chief Little Thunder, made no attempt to avoid Army retribution. Or possibly he was paralyzed with indecision. He waited Harney's coming with only the 250 braves who had destroyed Grattan's unit. For once, the Army outnumbered its opponents.

Harney gave the Brulés a token ultimatum on 3 September. When he left the fort, he had said, 'By God, I'm for battle. No peace'. Not surprisingly, he did not wait for an answer but fell on the village. His infantry and cavalry advanced in a quick pincers movement of two columns. The fury of their charge so surprised the Sioux, overconfident after their easy victory over Grattan, that they fled after only a slight resistance. Revenge was complete. Harney killed 85 warriors. Counting women and children, the dead totaled more than 100. He took four braves as prisoner-hostages and rounded up 70 women and children. His own losses were but five dead and seven wounded. Small wonder that the Sioux, ever after, called Harney 'The Butcher.'

After this Battle of Ash Hollow, actually fought at Blue Water Creek west of that Emigrant Trail camping ground toward Grattan's battle field, Harney moved up the California-Oregon Trail to talk to the Sioux at Fort Laramie. He told them to stay away from the White Man's Road—or else. He demanded that Indian robbers and murderers surrender. Several chiefs and warriors, including Spotted Tail, gave themselves up and were locked away in Fort Leavenworth.

The bellicose colonel suspended all trade with the Sioux, then marched smack through the heart of the Dakotas' country, inviting a brawl. But there were no takers. He circled the Sioux holy land, the Black Hills, and descended the White River to winter at Fort Pierre. In March of 1856

Right: Artist Charles M Russell documented a familiar incident on Montana's grassy plains – an Indian scouting party on a bluff awaiting the approach of whites unaware of their presence.

at that old fur trade 'factory' he exacted a peace treaty from the Tetons that reiterated and confirmed Fitzpatrick's document of 1851.

Harney had punished only the Tetons. The Cheyennes continued to annoy Overland Trail travelers. So the Army called upon another tough old soldier to lead a company against them. He was 60-year-old Colonel Edwin Vose Sumner.

Ironically, the veteran Indian fighter, commanding officer of Fort Leavenworth, was Harney's worst enemy or, at least, rival. Made a brevet colonel in 1840 for distinguished Florida service, Harney was promoted to Colonel of the Second Dragoons before the Mexican War, making him the nation's ranking cavalry officer. However, he clashed with General Winfield S Scott, Commanding General of the Army. Scott thought him too impetuous; for his part, the dragoon sized up Scott as weak-willed.

Scott replaced Harney with his own favorite, Sumner. Harney refused to step down and appealed to higher-ups. Finally, Harney won and Sumner lost. The former was restored to command of the 2nd Dragoons. But the latter performed well in the Mexican War, earning the brevet of brigadier general and the nickname of Bull, or Old Bull. Originally, it was Bull Head. The name was awarded him after his thick skull turned back a spent Mexican musket ball at the Battle of Cerro Gordo.

Sumner's two-pronged expedition caught the Cheyennes on the **Solomon River** of western Kansas on 29 July 1857. So overconfident were the 300 warriors that they waited in a European-type line of battle. This rare choice of tactics, an open encounter, was the result of a medicine man's assuring them that, after bathing their hands in a sacred lake, the warriors would be immune from bullets.

Old Bull Sumner had exactly the same number of fighting men as the Cheyennes. He had his men sling their carbines and led them in what was probably both the first and the last saber charge in Indian wars history, movies to the contrary. Either the soothsayer's super-natural vision was cloudy or the warriors had broken a taboo, for their spirit allies failed them. The spell was no more effective against musket balls than sabre cuts. The shaken Indians broke and ran for their lives, so fast that they lost only nine braves in a major psychological defeat. Only two of the cavalrymen, who pursued them with hacking sabres for the first seven miles of a headlong retreat, were killed. Sumner had ten enlisted men wounded and one officer, who was to become the Civil War's legendary J E B (Jeb) Stuart.

On balance, the brutal measures of the rivals, Harney and Sumner, probably saved both red and white lives in the long run. Their prompt and thorough punishment ended the Indians' contempt for the Army, fostered by Grattan's debacle. The conflict of cultures was so acute that war was inevitable, but for seven years there was a tacit ceasefire, an uneasy truce on the Great Plains. This shaky peace even survived the arrival of yet another wave of pioneers, those heading up the Smoky Hill Trail to Colorado, with 'Pike's Peak or Bust!' lettered on the canvas tops of their wagons.

The Stage is Set for Northwest Conflict

However long before the Pike's Peak Gold Rush of 1858, the infection of war spread all the way across the continent to Washington Territory. Isaac I Stevens, its young (35 years of age) and ambitious governor, doubled as superintendent of Indian affairs. He held a council in May and June of 1855 in the Walla Walla Valley. There he tried to persuade, then to pressure, the natives into peacefully abandoning much of their overlapping land claims for reservations of their own choosing around permanent villages or salmon fisheries.

The Nez Percés, always friendly to whites since they first shook Meriwether Lewis's hand in 1805, came in. So did their opposites, the Cayuses. The Yakimas, Walla Wallas and Umatillas showed up, too.

Old Peo-peo-mox-mox, chief of the Walla Wallas, told the governor that his people would not eat the white man's food in the great dining hall. Stevens, disappointed by the failure of his gustatory diplomacy, was shortly surprised by the general obstinacy of his guests. Though he promised chiefs annual salaries and homes, horses, cattle and even schools for their people, the Indians refused to give up their ancestral hunting and fishing grounds in exchange for the smaller sites that he was ready to assign them.

The governor then threatened them. Old Chief Joseph of the Nez Percés signed. To Stevens's satisfaction, the other chiefs followed suit. He was annoyed when Looking Glass of the Nez Percés, a late arrival, exclaimed, 'My people, what have you done! While I was away, you have sold my country!' But Stevens was able to cajole most of the tribal leaders by assuring them that they would not have to move for two or three years, since the Senate would debate that long before ratifying the treaty. The Indians misjudged the slippery Stevens badly. Stevens was a deceptive negotiator, indeed an outright liar—the type of individual that Indians would refer to as one who spoke with a forked tongue. He did not wait two years as he promised, but hardly two weeks, before declaring the Indian lands open to white settlement. In the face of such betrayal, the Indians' reaction of righteous indignation and anger seemed wholly justified.

War Breaks out with the Yakimas

Some Yakimas protested that Kamiakin had had no right to speak for them in accepting a reservation and giving up claims to land beyond its limits, or in permitting whites to build roads across their lands.

A Yakima War broke out in September of 1855 after exasperated young braves, including Kamiakin's nephew, Qualchin, murdered prospectors heading for British Columbia's gold fields. Next, they brutally murdered their well-liked agent, A J Bolon, when he investigated the killings. The Indians feared that he was fetching the Army to punish them.

Kamiakin was a pro-peace chief, though he wanted the whites to stay west of the Cascades. But he was easily able, with 500 warriors, to turn back a reconnaissance in strength from Fort Dalles. Major Granville O Haller lost five dead and 17 wounded on 6 October, then had to fight his way back to the fort after burying his howitzer and burning baggage and supplies to keep them from Yakima hands. Major, alias 'General', Gabriel Rains's Yakima Expedition did little more in November than burn a Catholic mission when they found gunpowder buried in its garden. But Colonel James Kelly's volunteers, by seizing Peo-peo-mox-mox during a parley, guaranteed the spread of war from Yakimas to Walla Wallas, and even Umatillas and

Above: After apprenticeship-like explorations of Minnesota with the French scientist, Nicollet, and a survey of the lower Des Moines River, **John Charles Frémont** was sent to explore the Rocky Mountains or, rather, the headwaters of the Platte River in 1842. From South Pass, he headed northwestward into the Wind River Mountains of the Rockies and climbed **Fremont Peak** in Wyoming, at 13,730 feet one of the highest peaks in the entire chain. When his report and map were published by Congress, the public began to be aware of the 'Pathfinder.'

Right: **Frémont** was a split personality, a splendid scientific explorer, but a failure as a soldier-politician. He reached the Rockies in 1842, the Great Basin and Oregon in 1843, and made a rash midwinter crossing of the Sierra Nevada into California. His reports of his great circuit excited much popular interest. He was back in California in 1845 but retired 'growlingly' to Oregon before a Mexican force. Surprised by Indians there, he retaliated against the wrong tribe. Frémont joined the Bear Flag rebels against Mexico and in the Mexican War formed his company, plus mountain men, into a California Battalion of 'horse marines' under Commodore Stockton rather than the Army. He accepted the surrender of California, to the annoyance of his superiors, and sided with the Navy in its controversy with General Kearny as to who was in supreme command. Kearny took him East for court martial for disobedience of orders. Found guilty, he was pardoned by the president but angrily resigned his commission. His private winter expedition to the San Juan Mountains for a railroad route was a disaster. Frémont later operated gold mines in California, ran for president, was a mediocre Civil War general, and Governor of Arizona Territory.

Cayuses, for they killed the chief and sent his scalp and ears to the Oregon settlements to be put on display.

By now, whites were shooting Indians on sight, as if they were predatory animals, and braves fell on the nearest settlers, usually innocent of wrongdoing, in their blind retaliation. Bewildered Army regulars, expecting to guard settlers from attack, often found themselves protecting peaceful Indians from bloodthirsty militiamen. Naturally, the embittered settlers preferred to muster their own militia companies to deal, decisively, with the Indians. They felt that they could not count on the ambivalent Army. They considered its commander virtually a traitor to his country.

Feisty General John E Wool, commanding the Department of the Pacific, was a veteran of 42 years service. He had not liked the indecent Cherokee Removal of the 1830s, which he had been forced by duty to supervise, and he would not tolerate now the machinations of the supposedly patriotic 'war governors', Stevens of Washington Territory and George Curry of Oregon Territory. He disliked the latter, but detested the former, considering Stevens to be a scoundrel. And he said so, publicly, openly sympathizing with the Indians and condemning the white citizenry as hot heads who wished to exterminate the natives. Wool ordered his subordinates not to fight Indians unless forced to do so, but to persuade all tribes to be peaceful.

Stevens blasted Wool for 'locking up' the regulars in their forts while hostiles killed citizens with impunity. He demanded the General's removal from command for incapacity and criminal neglect of duty.

Wool retorted that both 'war governors' were covetous men provoking needless bloodshed in order to prosper not only from Indian plunder, but from looting the US Treasury of militia pay and supplies and, eventually, reparations for war losses, real or imaginary. He was also profoundly disgusted, he said, by the brutal, disgraceful behavior of the volunteers against the two territories' peaceable Indians. Reluctantly, in order to protect innocent victims of war, white and red alike, Wool was forced to send Colonel George H Wright, the veteran now commanding Fort Dalles, to the front with 500 regulars. It was a bloodless campaign; all hostiles had scattered by mid-June of 1856. But Colonel B F Shaw's volunteers on 17 July thrashed 300 of the allied hostiles in the Grande Ronde Valley. He killed 40 and destroyed the village while losing only five dead and four wounded.

Peace in the Columbia Basin was more the work of Wright than Shaw, however. He persuaded Stevens to pull out his vengeful volunteers and the Indians ceased their disavowal of treaties, relinquished tribal lands and ceased hostilities. The Yakima War, or at least its beginnings,

Left: **Winfield Scott** was long lived for his days. Born in Virginia in 1786, just after the American Revolution, he died 80 years later in 1866, just after the close of the Civil War. The career soldier attended William and Mary College and began his military career as a militia officer, but in 1808 he was commissioned a captain of light artillery in the Regular Army and served on the Louisiana frontier. In the War of 1812, Scott distinguished himself at Queenstown Heights (1812) but was taken prisoner. He was exchanged and won fame in the Battles of Chippewa and Lundy's Lane in 1814 and was made a brigadier general. Congress and his home state of Virginia gave him medals and he was made a brevet major general. After he studied military tactics in Europe, he wrote a manual of infantry field exercises and maneuvers. He then served in the Black Hawk War (1832), commanded the forces in the Second Seminole War, and supervised the exile of the Cherokees from the south in 1838. Scott became Commanding General of the Army in 1841 on the death of General Alexander Macomb. In the Mexican War he was at first shunted aside as a Whig by the Democratic administration. Finally, Old 'Fuss and Feathers,' as his troops knew him from his love of showy uniforms, was given his head. He not only struck at the capital from Vera Cruz, he did so with many soldiers 'borrowed' from rival Zachary Taylor's force in the North. He captured Mexico City but was recalled in 1848 in another political squabble. Lieutenant General Scott was a national hero in the 1850s, though his presidential run was unsuccessful in 1852. The able Scott helped settle a San Juan Islands boundary dispute with Great Britain in Washington Territory's Puget Sound in 1859, but was really too old when the Civil War broke. He organized the defenses of Washington, but retired in 1861, to be succeeded by General George B McClellan.

seemed to fade away in November 1856. Forts Simcoe and Walla Walla were established to keep the peace in the Pacific Northwest. However, Stevens had the last laugh on Wool. He won his fight, getting the General reassigned in May of 1857.

The Yakimas were not yet ready to move onto a reservation for good, as had the Rogues. Some of their belligerents picked off farmers and Colville District miners while Kamiakin secretly sought alliances with the Palouses, Coeur d'Alenes and Spokanes against the 'white-eyes.'

The Army became exasperated in 1858 by the murder of miners, so in May, Lieutenant Colonel Edward J Steptoe marched from Fort Walla Walla to pacify the recalcitrant Yakimas and Coeur d'Alenes, hence the alternative name for part two of the Yakima War, the Coeur d'Alene War. (It was even called the Spokane War by some.) Steptoe took three dragoon companies, reinforced by an infantry unit and a few Nez Percé scouts, plus an artillery battery of two howitzers. He had only 164 men and each carried only 40 rounds of ammunition.

The Coeur d'Alenes were traditionally friendly to whites but, punished by white diseases, Stevens's treaties and the rush of aggressive miners to Colville, they walked into the waiting arms of the Spokanes and Yakimas in 1858.

Steptoe was bound for Colville. He never made it. To his shock, he found the grassy-hilled country called The Palouse (for its Indians) to be aswarm with war parties. There were 1200 Yakimas, Spokanes, Palouses and Coeur d'Alenes, all mounted.

When chiefs rode up to his camp one evening and ordered him away, Steptoe meekly—and wisely—obeyed. But his prudence went unrewarded. The Indians fell on the rear of his column as he turned back on 17 May 1858. All morning long they drew blood. He took up a defensive position on a hill, **Steptoe Butte**, from which he had to fight his way down to a ravine and back for water. Surrounded and pinned to his position, Steptoe fought well but, by dark, he had lost six dead, two of them officers, and a dozen men wounded. There were only three rounds of ammunition left per man.

Steptoe wanted to fight to the death but younger and cooler heads persuaded him to live to fight another day. Burying the dead and forfeiting the howitzers, the soldiers slipped away in the darkness and got themselves and their wounded comrades safely back to Fort Walla Walla.

The Army, smarting from the humiliation of Steptoe's aborted campaign, now sent Wright into action again. The Indian allies awaited him at Four Lakes on 1 September 1858. He chased some of the 500 warriors out of the pines with howitzer fire, then gave them a dose of musketry in the

Right: **Jefferson Davis** is commonly remembered only as president of the Confederate States of America during the Civil War. But he enjoyed a long career in United States government service before he played a leading role in states' rights and Secession, especially between 1861 and 1865. He was born in Kentucky in 1808 and educated at Transylvania University in Lexington. He graduated from West Point in 1828. Davis served for seven years at various frontier Army posts and saw action in the Black Hawk War with the Sauks and Foxes in 1832. He left the Army in 1835, the year that he married Zachary Taylor's daughter (who lived only a few more months), for the life of a Mississippi cotton planter. Davis entered Democratic politics in 1843 but in 1846 resigned from the House of Representatives to lead a volunteer regiment of Mississippi Rifles in the Mexican War from 1846 to 1848. Colonel Davis distinguished himself at the Siege of Monterrey and the Battle of Buena Vista, then returned home to his Mississippi plantation to recover from his war wounds. His interest in the West – both positive and negative – continued. He fought the admission of California to the Union as a free state. As Secretary of War for President Franklin Pierce he was the prime mover behind the important Pacific Railroad Surveys of 1853-54 and the subsequent building of a transcontinental railway (1869) that connected California with 'the States' but split, forever, not only buffalo herds but also Indian tribes into two great north and south segments. Naturally, he preferred and recommended the southern route, along the 32nd degree of latitude, and favored the Gadsden Purchase of 45,535 square miles for ten million dollars and cancellation of some Mexican claims against the US. This secured the Mesilla Valley of New Mexico and added the Gila River country to Arizona Territory in 1853. Davis was modest, fearless and honest and he always thought of himself as a soldier.

Above: The Army's General John E Wool did not want a fight with the Northwest Indians in the 1850s, but violence came anyway. Colonel **Benjamin F Shaw** (left) took his 2nd Regiment of Washington Territorial Militia on a march to Walla Walla against allied tribes. The campaign of 1856 was largely bloodless till July, when Shaw struck in Grande Ronde Valley in northeastern Oregon Territory and defeated them.

open. His men were armed with the new 1855 model 'rifled muskets' (that is, rifles), not smoothbores. They took the new hollow, conical, Minié balls which extended their effective range from 600 yards to almost 1000 yards. And the new slugs were capable of tearing through the toughest —and most sacred—buffalo-hide shields.

Now Major William Grier shouted 'Charge the rascals!' and his four companies of dragoons tore into the Indians, who fled with a loss of 60 dead and many more wounded. Incredibly, Wright did not have a man even hurt in the **Battle of Four Lakes**.

On 5 September at **Spokane Plain**, or Great Spokane Prairie, Wright repeated his bloody lesson. The grass fire started by the Indians provided a handy smoke screen for his yelling dragoons to charge and scatter 500 hostiles. Their loss could not be determined, but Wright had only one man wounded and a number of soldiers completely exhausted.

As the several whipped tribes made peace overtures, Wright policed the area, slaughtering 900 Palouse ponies. He then went after the ringleaders, hanging 15 of them and putting others in irons. For years, the pile of whitening horse bones on the Spokane River served not only as a landmark

but as a reminder of Army retribution for Steptoe's defeat.

Kamiakin was badly injured at Spokane Plain by a tree limb dropped on him by a howitzer round. He got across the line into Canada, however. In 1861 he sneaked back into southeast Washington Territory and lived quietly near Spokane. He died at Rock Lake in 1877.

Kamiakin's brother-in-law, Owhi, came in to make peace and was forced, under threat of death, to summon his son, Qualchin, whose murders had started the war. Wright had him summarily hanged. Owhi tried to escape by lashing a lieutenant in the face with a horsewhip, but the officer shot him three times in the body and a sergeant gave him the *coup de grace*, a fourth shot in the head.

To the south, trouble had broken out in Oregon as early as 1851. The ten founders of Port Orford on the south coast had hardly waded ashore in July before they were attacked. They holed up atop an unusual, whale-shaped, offshore 'stack', Battle Rock. A hundred braves charged the rock at low tide, clambering up its steep sides as their friends filled the air with arrows. J M Kirkpatrick and his men struck back fiercely with a round from their antique ship's cannon. An estimated 20 warriors were killed and 17 more wounded. But since the defenders had only two more charges for the gun, they hoarded them for 14 days of siege, then sneaked ashore at dark and cut through the woods to Portland.

Hostilities shifted inland to the Siskiyou Trail area of the Rogue River in southern Oregon, named for the villainous Indians who had a reputation for ambushing travelers. Captain Andrew Jackson Smith commanded a solitary troop of dragoons at Fort Lane to keep the Rogues in subjection in 1855. In October, when rumors of war spread Smith moved some peaceful Indian men up to the fort for their own protection. Before the women and children could follow them, their camp was raided by a volunteer company. The amateur soldiers killed 23 people, mostly women, children and old men. On the very next day, the young warriors took their revenge, but they fell on the wrong persons, butchering 27 innocent Rogue River settlers.

Newspapers and the public joined in a clamor for Indian scalps. In fact, they wanted the complete destruction of the 'bloody fiends'. Just as Wool had predicted, the raid-and-retaliation cycle in Oregon blazed up into a full-scale war of extermination by both sides.

When Wool reluctantly sent regulars to reinforce the volunteers in the spring of 1856, the Rogues agreed to surrender to Captain Smith, whom they trusted. But they changed their minds and decided to destroy him. Some 200 Rogue Rivers attacked Smith's 50 horsemen and 30 foot soldiers at **Big Meadow** on the Rogue.

Fortunately for the captain, two Indian women wanted no part of the upcoming bloodbath. They warned him of the treachery of chiefs Old John, Limpy and George. Smith had time to dig in atop a hill before the attack came on the morning of 27 May 1856. His howitzer and the infantry's musket fire did considerable damage but his dragoons' short-range musketoons or carbines were less effective. The regulars appeared doomed by the great discrepancy in strength between themselves and the Indians. Old John sensing victory cursed the whites in his own tongue and his lieutenants shook hangman's nooses at them. The two Indian women dutifully translated Old John's fiery speech for Smith.

Just in the very nick of time, Captain Christopher C

Augur's company of regulars came up on the double. The Rogues, pressed between two forces, ran. Smith's men, though almost out of both ammunition and water, managed a gallant and spirited counter-attack as Augur came in view. When the warriors lit out, they took their dead and wounded so their casualties could not be known. But Smith lost nine killed and 17 wounded, Augur two dead and three wounded.

A month after Big Meadows, completely dispirited, the Rogues surrendered and allowed themselves to be herded like sheep onto the coastal Siletz Reservation, protected by Siletz Blockhouse, a satellite of Fort Hoskins. There they nearly starved in the next months. Old John was exiled to the military prison at Fort Alcatraz in the middle of San Francisco Bay.

Comanches and Texas Rangers Clash on the South Plains

During the pre-Civil War decade, Kiowas and Comanches continued their old tradition of raiding Mexicans, but largely left Arkansas River and Santa Fe Trail travelers alone. They did not wish to jeopardize their presents of arms and ammunition ('for hunting', of course) from the *Anglos*. But they eventually strayed from the Great Comanche War Trail to Mexico and stole livestock from West Texans.

A new governor in 1858, Hardin R Runnels, admitted that it would be cheaper for the state just to pay raided frontiersmen for their stolen cows and jackasses. But he was determined to rebuild the Texas Rangers after a decade of decline, and used the border troubles to justify his call-up of new men.

Runnels chose the best man available since John Coffee Hays, the greatest of the Rangers, had migrated to California in the Gold Rush. Senior Captain John S (Rip) Ford was told to cooperate with General David E Twiggs's regulars and with US Indian agents. But in typical Texan fashion, Runnels also instructed him to brook no interference from them or anyone else. His orders were clear, simple and specific: 'Follow any and all trails of hostiles or suspected hostile Indians you may discover and, if possible, overtake and chastize them, if unfriendly'. He wanted the most summary punishment for the enemies of Texas.

Ford intended to strike the Comanches hard. If he did not secure a telling victory, he was prepared to accept a disastrous defeat. But half-way measures were unthinkable. And he would not be restrained by the supposedly sacrosanct Indian Territory border.

On 29 April Ford left Texas by crossing the Red River. One day, some of his Keechi, Tonkawa, Shawnee and Anadarko scouts from the Brazos Reserve, led by the Indian Agent's son, Shapley P Ross, killed a buffalo with fresh Comanche arrows in it. On 11 May 1858, they spotted a small village near the Canadian River and Oklahoma's Antelope Hills. At seven o'clock the next morning, Rip Ford loosed his scouts. They demolished the five lodges, mounted the Comanches' horses and joined the Ranger pursuit of two braves for three miles. From there, the Tonks and Texans could see the conical white lodges of a much bigger village three miles away on the Cherokee side of the Canadian.

Chief Iron Jacket, who wore an old coat of Spanish mail, was alerted and ready for the Rangers. Trusting to his armor's medicine, he led the force bearing down on Ford. But a half-dozen musket balls dropped his horse, and Shawnee and Anadarko guides riddled the chief on the ground. A number of individual fights occupied an area of six by three miles. Mostly, Rangers and reservation Indians made futile chases of Comanches who only occasionally would halt and fight. When the chief replacing Iron Jacket was also shot down by the Captain of Ford's Shawnees, the Comanches gave up the field. Ford recalled, 'Our red allies sent up a wild shout of triumph'. Only the weakened condition of their horses prevented a pursuit by the Texans.

When Comanches rallied from another camp a few miles up the Canadian, Ford let his allies handle it. He described the colorful scene: 'With yells and menaces and every species of insulting gesture and language, they tried to excite the Reserve Indians into some act of rashness by which they could profit. . . . Shields and lances and bows and headdresses, prancing steeds. . . . When the combatants rushed at each other with defiant shouts, nothing save the piercing report of the rifle varied the affair from a battlefield of the Middle Ages.'

The 100 Rangers grew tired of the pageant after a half-hour of this cavorting without damage to either side. They

Above: **Lieutenant Colonel (later Brigadier General) Silas Casey**, CO of Fort Steilacoom during the Indian troubles in Washington Territory. Fort Steilacoom was situated on the shore of Puget Sound, ten miles southwest of Tacoma.

moved in and drove the Comanches from the field. All fighting was over because Ford's tired horses could not manage an attack on Buffalo Hump's big village, only a dozen miles away. Ford engaged 300 warriors in the drawn out and intermittent seven-hour battle. He killed 76 warriors, captured 300 horses, and took 18 prisoners, mostly women and children. His force suffered only two dead and two wounded.

Ford commended Agent Ross and also his own four captains. Of the latter he said, 'They behaved under fire in a gallant and soldier-like manner, and I think they have fully vindicated their right to be recognized as Texas Rangers of the old stamp.'

Runnels was pleased when First Sergeant Robert Cotter sent him a souvenir of Ford's victory, accompanied by a note—'I send you . . . a small part of the Comanche chief's coat of mail. It covered his body and each piece lapped over like shingles on a roof. It is all I could get, as it was eagerly taken and divided by the boys.'

Rush Springs and Crooked Creek

That summer, the Army followed the Rangers' example and went on the offensive after too long a time on the defensive in a line of 13 forts spaced for 400 miles across West Texas. Secretary of War Jeff Davis's favorite Indian fighter was appointed leader of the expedition. Captain (Brevet Major) Earl Van Dorn was brave, gentle, and kind, but he was also a hard-drinking, boastful adulterer, according to California's Judge Charles Fernald.

Van Dorn's column, the **Wichita Expedition**, was composed of four companies of the 2nd Cavalry, 135 Indians and a guard detachment of infantry to watch over campsites. Oddly, the commander of the Indian scouts was the Agent's 20-year-old son, Lawrence S (Sul) Ross, home on vacation from college. Van Dorn set up a supply base, on Otter Creek near the Wichita Mountains and, once he located Comanches, made a 90-mile march in 37 hours.

Van Dorn reconnoitered the little valley of Rush Creek

and found Buffalo Hump and 500 of his followers in 120 lodges at the springs. At sunrise, 1 October 1858, Van Dorn's 350 men struck. His surprise attack was perfect; he separated braves from their ponies and he got men in among the teepees. But the **Battle of Rush Springs** was a ferocious one, for the Comanches stood to defend their families.

In the series of desperate hand-to-hand engagements, Sul Ross fell with a bullet in his side. A Comanche grabbed at him to lift his scalp, but a lieutenant planted a charge of buckshot in the Indian's spine. Van Dorn was shot in the wrist and stomach with arrows.

The Army killed 56 warriors (and, accidentally, two women) and dispersed the rest in the hour-and-a-half battle. Some 300 horses were captured and all 120 lodges burned. Van Dorn had five dead and a dozen men wounded, including himself. No wonder General Twiggs crowed that it was 'a victory more decisive and complete than any recorded in the history of our Indian warfare.'

Van Dorn was not expected to live although the army

surgeon extracted the arrow from his abdomen. But he was as tough as he was vain, and was back in the saddle in only five weeks. On 13 May 1859 he surpassed his Rush Springs fight by trapping a Comanche war party at **Crooked Creek** near the Cimarron River. He utterly destroyed the Comanches who, he reported, fought till not one was left to bend a bow. Not one brave escaped; 49 were dead and the five wounded and 32 women became prisoners. Van Dorn lost two troopers and four Indian scouts; two officers and nine enlisted men were wounded.

The Pyramid Lake War

The last major campaign in the West before the Civil War broke out was the Paiute War, or Pyramid Lake War, of 1860 in that part of Utah Territory then called Washoe rather than Nevada. The discovery of Comstock silver led to the murders of miners around Virginia City which were blamed on both Washoes and Paiutes. But war did not blaze up until two Paiute girls were brutally raped by whites at Williams Station. Paiutes rescued the girls, killed the rapists and burned the stage station.

This **Williams Station Massacre** led to the formation of a citizens' army under Major William Ormsby. He was a poor soldier and led his rag-tag army of miners into a trap at the Big Bend of the Truckee River just south of Pyramid Lake. This trap was set by Numaga, a pro-peace chief dragged into belligerence after a fast against violence. As a Sacramento *Union* correspondent wrote about Ormsby's force, 'They had charged through an open gate into an Indian corral.' Numaga let the terrified volunteers retreat in a wild run that turned into a sagebrush gauntlet. Some historians, such as Ferol Egan, have likened the rout to a bloody rabbit drive.

California rushed militia units to the rescue of its under-populated neighbor. The **Carson Valley Expedition**, a handful of regulars, joined them, and ex-Texas Ranger Jack Hays took command of a provisional Washoe Regiment. His skirmish at Big Meadows near the Big Bend of the Carson River was inconclusive. But he pushed across Ormsby's battlefield and struck the Paiutes at Pinnacle Mountain. Hays killed 25 warriors and captured 20 ponies before scattering the Indians to the desert winds. They never regrouped for resistance after Fort Churchill was

Left: Artist James E Taylor and engraver Charles Spiegel titled this engraving **Sam Cherry's Last Shot**. Colonel Richard I Dodge was Adjutant when the Army established Fort Davis in West Texas in 1855 with six companies of the Eighth US Infantry. From October 10-30, Dodge was out with a tiny patrol, only a single non-commissioned officer, three privates and the scout, Cherry, to find timber suitable for saw logs. They found Indian signs everywhere but not of large parties, so the men were careful but not uneasy. At the end of the month, Dodge was replaced on muster day by Sergeant Love. That night the party did not return. An infantry company hurried out and found the soldiers, riddled with bullets and disfigured. At the entrance to the *cañón* of the Limpia River, called Wild Rose Pass, about 30 mounted Indians had apparently cut them off from any retreat to the fort, driving the troopers into a trap from which Cherry tried to escape. He was found, pinned to the ground by his dead horse, but unscalped and not mutilated, his pistol still in his hand. Dodge immediately understood why. Indians feared suicides and would not scalp – even touch – one. When Cherry's horse broke its leg and fell on him, Sam Cherry shot five of his pursuers but put the last lead slug into his own head.

Over: **Scalp Dance of the Sioux** by George Catlin.

established at the Big Bend of the Carson to keep a watchful eye on them.

Arizona Territory had been surprisingly quiet in the 1850s. Apaches continued to raid their age-old enemies, the Mexicans, but hardly ever took on the better-armed Americans. In fact, for three solid years, the Butterfield Overland Mail Line's Concord coaches of the Mesilla-Tucson run passed through the very heart of the Chiricahua country, the defile of Apache Pass at the north end of the Chiricahua Mountains, without problems. Indeed, some Chiricahuas regularly traded firewood for supplies at the mail station.

The situation in Arizona changed almost overnight in 1860 because of the stupidity of a single army lieutenant. In October, Apaches hit the adobe ranch house of a roughneck settler, John Ward, on Sonoita Creek. They not only stole his cattle, they abducted one of his children, his stepson and adopted son, Félix Téllez. Félix was the 12-year-old son of Ward's Mexican wife and an Apache father, born while she was a captive.

Ward was away at the time of the raid, but on his return he firmly identified Cochise, chief of the Chiricahuas, as the guilty party from descriptions by eye-witnesses. The chief was hard to miss; neat and well-mannered, six feet tall with muscular shoulders, a barrel chest and arrow-straight posture. One settler described him as 'As fine a looking Indian as one ever saw.'

Ward complained at Fort Buchanan, 40 miles south of Tucson, and the courageous but reckless Second Lieutenant George N Bascom of the 7th Infantry was ordered to restore the kidnapped boy to him. He took 54 men on mules and pitched his tent near the Apache Pass stage station where Cochise often camped. Bascom invited the chief to a talk on 4 February 1861.

Cochise assumed that it was a routine meeting, so he brought five members of his family—a brother, two nephews, a woman and a child. At first he thought that the short-fused lieutenant must be joking when he demanded the return of the boy and the livestock. Cochise denied any complicity in the raid and guessed that Coyoteros, or White Mountain Apaches, were responsible. He offered to help ransom the boy and recover the animals. But Bascom would have none of it; he had convinced himself of the chief's guilt. He bluntly advised him that he was under arrest and that the tent was surrounded by a dozen soldiers. Cochise barely waited for the interpreter to explain Bascom's treachery before he had his knife out. But he did not kill the lieutenant; instead, he slashed his way through the tent's wall. His kin were seized as hostages but Cochise escaped.

Cochise quickly took several whites prisoner on the

Below: Right after Adobe Walls (1874), scout **Amos Chapman** protected a wounded comrade in the Buffalo Wallow fight.

Butterfield Trail, for bargaining power. He did not bother with the Mexicans he despised. When he captured eight teamsters, he just tied the Mexicans to the wheels of their wagons and set the vehicles afire.

Reinforced by White Mountain warriors and the Warm Springs braves of his giant father-in-law, Mangas Coloradas, Cochise appeared under a flag of truce. Bascom suspected treachery—and he was right. He would not budge, but three stage employees walked out to talk with their old friend, Cochise. The Indians tossed aside their white flag and seized one of them, James F Wallace. The other men ran. Both were hit, and one later died. Bascom's troopers returned the Apache fire.

On 6 February Cochise shouted an offer to trade hostages. Bascom was willing, but wanted the Téllez lad and the livestock thrown in. Cochise repeated his offer of a trade, this time in writing. He attached a note, written for him by Wallace, to a stake that he drove into the ground in view of the stage station.

When Bascom took no action, Cochise lost his temper. He had his men pile up heaps of tinder-dry brush in the canyon road to halt and seize the stages. But before he could light it, the westbound stage crashed through, ahead of schedule.

Cochise turned his attention to the eastbound coach. His men wounded the driver and killed one of the lead mules. The passengers cut the carcass from the harness and headed for the station. The Apaches had stripped the planking from the stringers of a small bridge, but the mules dragged the protesting stage over the span on its axles. At the far abutment, the wheels found purchase and, miraculously, the seemingly doomed stage clattered up to the besieged station.

Cochise ran off Bascom's mules, but paid a price. Riflemen wounded up to a dozen of the rustlers. Bascom's courier brought a medical unit which, surprisingly, captured three Coyoteros. The arrival of two dragoon companies from Fort Breckinridge sent Cochise flying towards Mexico. Patrols searched the mountains around the re-opened pass, but encountered no hostiles.

But the handiwork of Cochise was everywhere. The charred corpses of the Mexican wagonmen were cut away from the wheels and buried. The horrible remains of Cochise's six American hostages were found, repeatedly lanced in Comanche fashion, and so butchered that Wallace, Cochise's particular friend, could only be identified by gold fillings in his teeth. About 16 Mexicans and Americans were tortured to death by Cochise between 4 and 11 February.

Keeping the woman and child in detention, Bascom, with the approval of his officers, on 11 February hanged the six Apache men to the limbs of scrub oaks over the graves of the murdered whites. And he refused to bury their remains. The corpses hung there, dessicating in the hot desert winds for months, a warning to all Apaches.

The warning was not heeded. Cochise and Mangas Coloradas terrified the territory. Within two months, more than 150 Americans and Mexicans were dead. On 10 August 1861 the *Arizonan* newspaper lamented that most of the territory's male population had been killed or run off and that most ranches, farms and mines had fallen to the Apaches. Even conservative estimates put the final cost of these Apache depredations at more than 4000 lives and hundreds of thousands of dollars in property losses.

Above: **James Butler (Wild Bill) Hickok,** 1837-1876, was a soldier and scout, but much more of a gambler, gunfighter and lawman. He was born in Illinois, but went to 'Bleeding Kansas' in 1855 where he was a teamster and stagecoach driver. He served in the Union Army during the Civil War but his activities remained cloaked in mystery. With his buckskins and long, Custer-like locks, Hickok soon became famous as a lawman. He was deputy US marshal at Fort Riley, Kansas, then he scouted for General Philip Sheridan for a time and even considered making a career as an Army scout. During this stint as a plainsman-scout, he was wounded in one arm (March 1868) during a skirmish with a Cheyenne war party. The injury was serious enough to require him to return to his boyhood home in Troy Grove, Illinois, to recuperate. When he returned to the Plains, it was not as a scout but as a guide for a hunting party of Easterners. He was next acting-sheriff of Ellis County and town marshal of Hays City, Kansas. By 1871, he was marshal of Abilene, Kansas, at the end of the Chisholm Trail, and his army scouting days were over. He later played himself in one of William F (Buffalo Bill) Cody's Wild West shows, 'Scouts of the Plains,' then worked his way up to the Black Hills of South Dakota via Cheyenne, Wyoming, mostly as a card sharp. He was murdered by Jack McCall as he sat in a Deadwood poker game. The cards that Wild Bill was holding have come to be called the 'Dead Man's Hand' – aces and eights.

Below: Carl L Boeckmann painted the 8th Minnesota Mounted Infantry at the **Battle of Kildeer Mountain**, North Dakota, 1864, when General Alfred Sully broke the back of Santee and Teton Sioux resistance subsequent to the Minnesota Uprising of 1862.

INDIAN BATTLES DURING THE CIVIL WAR

When the echoes of Fort Sumter's bombardment rolled across the plains and mountains, Indians were not slow to fill the vacuum left by departing regulars. But militiamen rushed to fill the breach in the frontier's defenses. By war's end, 1865, the Volunteer Army in the West grew from 11,000 to almost 20,000. Officers varied widely in ability, just as in the Regular Army, but the militiamen were a surprise. Most were healthier specimens, and true patriots, who made better soldiers than those who clogged the ranks of the so-called peacetime Army. Even Confederate prisoners, 'Galvanized Yankees', volunteered to fight Indians. The civilized Indians of Oklahoma fought on both sides, but mainly in Arkansas, not in the Far West.

Wars in the Rockies and the Southwest

Two of the best leaders of citizen-soldiers of the Civil War in the West were Colonels Patrick Edward Connor and James H Carleton. The former, a pugnacious Irish immigrant, had been an 18-year-old enlisted man in the Seminole War, then a captain of volunteers in the Mexican War. In 1861 Governor John Downey of California appointed Connor colonel of the 3d California Infantry, to patrol the US mail route between Salt Lake City and California, protecting travelers and the new telegraph line as well as the mails with his 750 men.

But it was the Carleton who first drew blood. He had soldiered in Maine's hardly-bellicose Aroostook 'War' of 1838 before beginning a 20-year career in the regulars, where he rose to the rank of major of dragoons. He was the Governor's choice in 1861 for colonel of the 1st California Infantry.

Contemporaries called Carleton selfish, ambitious, tyrannical, aggressive, abrasive. He had thick moustache, eyebrows and sideburns, and liked to pose for photographers in Napoleonic posture. But he was a zealous and able officer, who replaced General E R S Canby as departmental commander in New Mexico and Arizona in 1862.

Early that year, Carleton led his California Column all the way to Fort Davis, Texas, retaking the Rio Grande forts for the Union. But Mangas Coloradas and Cochise mistakenly believed that Forts Buchanan, Breckinridge and Fillmore had been abandoned because of the Army's fear

Left: Peace loving **Chief Numaga** of Nevada's Paiutes was driven to war in 1860 by white violence.

of their warriors, not the threat of Rebel invasion. So Mangas, supported by Cochise, planned an ambush for Carleton, now a brigadier general, in the bottleneck of Apache Pass. The giant Mangas Coloradas, who towered over his tall son-in-law, Cochise, at six-foot-six, had been friendly with whites for years. But now annoyed by American miners at Silver City and Pinos Altos, he threw in his lot with Cochise's hostiles.

On 15 July 1862 Captain Thomas L Roberts led Carleton's lead company into the trap set by 'Red Sleeves'. Roberts was fired on from both slopes but had to press on to the spring because of his parched troopers. His two howitzers could lob a 7-pound shell 1000 yards, shrapnel 800 yards, and deadly canister shot 250 yards. The artillery shells cleared Apaches from the breastworks they had erected around the springs, but there were still perhaps 500 Indians in the pass. Roberts sent a warning message to Captain John C Cremony's supply train and cavalry escort, which were behind him. Mangas Coloradas and 50 warriors took off after Sergeant Mitchell's five couriers, who now rode for their very lives. Every man was hit, but none was shot from his saddle. Three of the horses were shot, throwing their riders. Two men were picked up, but Private John Teal was left behind, alone, to fight off the greatest war chief of the Southwest and his 50 picked warriors.

The Californian dropped down behind the carcass of his horse and commenced firing carefully with his breech-loading, repeating carbine. The Indians were puzzled, awed, by the rapid fire that the one soldier maintained. Repeaters were new to them. Instead of rushing him, they circled for an hour, not daring to come to close quarters. Recalled Teal, 'I got a good shot at a prominent Indian, and slipped a carbine bullet into his breast. He must have been a man of some note because, soon after, they seemed to get away from me.'

The 'man of some note' was Chief Mangas Coloradas. Unconscious, he was rescued by Cochise who did not trust his own tribal *curanderos* but took him all the way to Janos, Chihuahua, where a Mexican surgeon was forced to operate on him, under penalty of death if he failed to cure the chief. Mangas was out of action for months with his chest wound and was a strange sight when he returned to Arizona in a Mexican sombrero, serape and leather leggings—and Chinese sandals.

Carleton's main column reached Apache Pass ten days after the gutsy Teal hiked back to his comrades, not for-

Below: In 1862 Anton Gag painted a realistic view of the Sioux attacking **New Ulm** from the German colony's surrounding cornfields.

Above: Cheyenne **Little Wolf** with his peace pipe and his goateed captor, **Captain Clark** of the Second Cavalry.

getting to carry his saddle so that his pay would not be docked. To protect his exposed lines of communication and deny the area to Cochise and Mangas, Carleton founded Fort Bowie in Apache Pass.

Mangas returned to raiding but did not live long to enjoy his depredating. The Army resorted again to treachery to entrap and kill him. Such action was justified, in army eyes, by his record—'the most atrocious cruelties, the most vindictive revenges and widespread injuries ever perpetrated by an American Indian'. He was lured into an army camp near Pinos Altos on 17 January 1863 by the promise of a parley with Captain E D Shirland.

Mangas Coloradas was held at old abandoned Fort McLane on the Mimbres River. There, Private Clark Stocking overheard General Joseph R West, who looked like a pygmy alongside the chief, tell two sentries that the old 'murderer' had left a trail of blood for 500 miles. 'I want him "dead or alive", tomorrow morning. Do you understand?' he asked the guards, 'I want him *dead*.'

That bitter-cold night, a prospector, Daniel Conner, saw sentinels heat their bayonets in a campfire and stick them into the chief's legs and feet as he lay, rolled up in his blankets, by the fire. When he jumped up, the guards shot him, point blank, with their muskets and finished him off with six-shooters. One soldier scalped Mangas and, later, before he was buried, another cut off his head and boiled the flesh off to sell the skull to a phrenologist in the East. The wretched General West 'investigated' the incident. He claimed that the Apache was shot during his third attempt to escape and that the affair in no way compromised the good faith of the US Army.

The Shoshones (Shoshoni) of the Pacific Northwest had been friendly to Lewis and Clark and American mountain men, but relations with whites deteriorated and hit a low in 1862 when the Indians boldly marched down the street of Franklin, a hamlet in their winter camping grounds just above the Idaho line on Bear River. They wanted the settlement abandoned.

Colonel Connor was called in to discipline the Shoshones. He used a norther to hide his movements, leading 250–300 Californians through the blizzard. But Bear Hunter was ready to receive him on Bear River, 140 miles north of Bear Lake. In fact, he had added rock parapets to the natural defenses of his steep ravine.

On 27 January 1863, just as Connor's skirmishers deployed, they were dumbfounded to see a chief ride up and down in front of the gulch, brandishing a spear and chanting in quite recognizable English—'Fours right, fours left, come on you California sons of bitches!' Connor's men were more amused than intimidated by this strange performance and they speedily flanked the Shoshones' position, then swept through the village in the face of obstinate resistance as braves defended their wives and children.

Casualties were high for an Indian fight. Some of the braves had to be killed in their hiding places. Bear Hunter was one of 224 Indians killed, by Connor's count. But a Mormon tallied 400 bodies on the snow-covered field, many of them women and children.

The Battle of Bear River, almost forgotten today, won Connor his general's star as well as command of the Department of the Plains in 1865. And doubtless it saved the scalps of many prospectors. Connor was able to report that fall that all roads out of Utah could be traveled with safety. The Shoshones signed treaties in 1868 and 1873, went on the Fort Hall Reservation, and stayed there peacefully, except for a few young men who joined in the Bannock War of Chief Buffalo Horn in 1878.

War with the Eastern Sioux

When trouble came from the Sioux again, it arrived from an unexpected quarter. The sedentary Eastern Sioux, or Santees, were the least warlike people of that Indian nation. Some were Christians, all seemed submissive wards of government, accepting fatalistically reservation life on a strip of land along the Minnesota River. In 1851, by treaty, they had acknowledged the extension of US jurisdiction and had sold away their hunting grounds.

After the war, there would be no shortage of explanations for the savage uprising of a presumably peaceful native people. Some whites blamed the cutworms that ruined the Indians' spring corn crop and left them nearly starving. Others blamed the incessant pressure of settlers, both aggressive Anglo-Saxons and stolid, phlegmatic, Swedish and German immigrants who occupied one-time Santee land. Then there was the indifference or corruption of Indian agents, the meddling of missionaries and the chicanery of Indian traders. All these factors galled the Santee Sioux into deeper discontent.

As the Civil War wore on, rations fell short or were spoiled, unfit for human consumption. Blankets were cut in half to double their number. The monopolistic Indian trading posts, like company stores, got the Dakotas into debt, honestly and otherwise. When a war-distracted Washington was tardy in sending annuity payments to the agent at Yellow Medicine the Sioux feared that the traders would ask the Army to collect on these debts. Fort Ridgely tried to reassure uneasy Santees that its soldiers were not collection agents. But traders put signs on their counters advising their red customers that no more credit would be extended until the annuity should arrive and all outstanding debts were paid. When an interpreter protested that the Sioux might starve while waiting for Washington's bureaucrats to act, trader Andrew Myrick quipped, callously, 'If they're hungry, let 'em eat grass, or their own shit.'

The very day that elders sat to discuss their plight, 17 August 1862, four hungry hunters were making their way back to the reservation, disgusted at having shot no game. One of the frustrated youths dared another to prove his bravery by killing a white man. Before they were through with their senseless test of courage, five harmless settlers of Meeker County lay dead.

Little Crow, who had been the Santee chief since 1834, was a cautious man. A long-time peace advocate, he was held largely responsible by whites for the lack of hostilities ever since the 1851 treaty. But he was weak-willed, as easily swayed to war as to peace, though he had firmly placed his feet on 'the white man's road'. (He lived in a house, ran a farm, and had visited Washington while wearing a plug hat.) He was an opportunist without the courage of his convictions. Deep inside him remained some of the old irresponsibility and arrogance of his misspent youth. As a young man, he had been alcoholic, mendacious and adulterous. He had finally been 'invited' by cuckolded husbands to leave his own village, Pig's Eye, on the site of St Paul. His father described him then as a young man with very little sense. True, when he became chief, he changed his ways, at least in terms of drinking and womanizing.

In a stormy, all-night council, tribal elders heard Little Crow warn that war with the powerful whites was futile, then persuade himself that it was inevitable because of the murders. He took over the rebellion from the militant youngsters even though his initial strategy, an attack on Fort Ridgely before it could be reinforced, was overruled.

The Santees instead attacked small towns and Indian agencies. Their first victim was a clerk at the Redwood Agency, shot in cold blood although he was married to a Sioux. Stores and homes were burned as the raiders tried unsuccessfully to wipe out **New Ulm**. A small (46 man) party of volunteer soldiers from the fort then blundered into the Sioux. Only half of them escaped back to Ridgely.

At midnight of 18 August the first day of the undeclared war, Indians were looting their own stores at Yellow Medicine Agency as the blood clotted on the last of their 400 victims, murdered in unsuspecting settlements. As many as 300 refugees crowded into Fort Ridgely, the vanguard of perhaps 30,000 people who would choke the roads in their flight from an area 50 miles wide by 250 miles long.

Finally, Little Crow and his 800 war-painted warriors moved against the fort, which was crammed with non-combatants but held by only 155 volunteer infantry. Other war parties ranged widely about, killing all settlers that they found. At Lake Shetek, they massacred a party completely; there was not one survivor.

Minnesotans were praying for help from the bastion of the Old Northwest, St Paul's Fort Snelling. But Fort Ridgely was not counting on prayer. It sent Private William Sturgis for help. His dash of 125 miles in 18 hours would not be surpassed until the fabled ride of Portugee Philips, four years later.

While the alarm was being spread, Fort Ridgely had to hold against two assaults of several waves of Indians on 20 and 22 August. It did so only because of an accident, a fluke of circumstance. Though seriously undermanned in 1862, the fort had once been an ordnance depot. It retained a 24-pound cannon and a 6-pound and a 12-pound mountain howitzer.

Luckily, the artillery had been looked after by Ordnance Sergeant John Jones, who had also taken the time to train gun crews. Jones's canister shot at close quarters tore attackers to rags, while the big 24-pounder devastated Little Crow's headquarters in a ravine. The Sioux were demoralized by the cannon, saying that, given such 'wagon guns', they could rule the world. The Santees lost 100 men in the siege, mostly to the gun battery.

Colonel Henry Hastings Sibley was the choice of the governor of Minnesota to put down the uprising. The 51-year-old, Detroit-born, former fur trader was the Terri-

Left: George Catlin met **Steep Wind**, a Sans Arc (No Bows) Sioux at Fort Pierre, SD, during his trip up the Missouri River in 1832. Catlin was noted for his accuracy in the depiction of costumes and war paint.

Below left: Catlin painted **Black Dog** of the Santee Sioux c. 1835 when that tribe was still peaceable. It would later be responsible for the horrors of the Minnesota Uprising in 1862.

Below: Robert Lidneaux painted a version of what was probably the worst massacre in American history, that of **Sand Creek, Colorado**. On 29 November 1864, Colonel John M Chivington took his revenge for the murders of many miners and settlers by Southern Cheyennes and Arapahos emboldened by the absence of the Regular Army during the Civil War. Chivington was called the Fighting Parson because he was a minister who spurned a chaplaincy, saying that he wanted a fighting commission, not a praying one. He was the hero of the Battle of Glorieta Pass, New Mexico, in which the Confederate invasion of the Southwest was turned back. He led 700 Colorado Volunteers through the snow from Fort Lyon to fall on Black Kettle's sleeping camp of 500 Cheyennes and a few Arapahos on a bitter-cold dawn. Chivington ignored the white flag and Stars and Stripes that Black Kettle, thinking himself under the protection of Fort Lyon, quickly raised as a sign of peace. The Coloradans killed, and in many cases mutilated, 200 Indian men, women and children indiscriminately. The Chief escaped. Colorado was pleased by Chivington's brutal action but a Congressional committee denounced him. He resigned his commission but bore the stigma of the massacre for the rest of his life.

torial Delegate to Congress who organized the Minnesota Territory and brought about the Santee land cession in 1851 and was, in 1857, the state's first governor.

Sibley took a relief column out of Fort Snelling as soon as possible. But he knew that it was inadequate. While in the village of St Peter, he received a cry for help from New Ulm, being attacked again. But he could not spare any men till reinforcements should arrive. On 23 August the Santees hit New Ulm, dashing through the streets to plunder and fire buildings till one-third of the town was gone. But citizens of other settlements made common cause with the Germans of New Ulm and repulsed the Sioux by nightfall.

Once reinforcements brought his troop strength to 1600, Sibley marched to Fort Ridgely, which was full of sick, wounded and dead. He had to bury the corpses outside the fort for reasons of sanitation, but the graves detail was attacked. All but one of the horses drawing the wagons were killed. The burial party fought back from behind wagons and dead animals, but 23 men were killed before a relief column drove off the Santee Sioux.

Fort Ridgely was badly battered, but its brave defense closed the door on any Sioux advance down the Minnesota River to threaten St Paul itself. Chief Big Eagle later observed that if the Santees had crushed the fort, nothing could have stopped them short of the Mississippi River.

Already, some Santee chiefs were arguing whether to flee westward, surrender, or stand and fight. Some wanted to kill all white prisoners, too. The decision was to fight, but to spare the hostages.

Sibley started up the Minnesota River Valley for Yellow Medicine and on 23 September, when in sight of the agency, was attacked at **Wood Lake** by Little Crow and 700 men. Once again the Sioux showed that they had no stomach for artillery. Little Crow later said that he was ashamed to be a Dakota because the 'wagon guns' of the whites, whom he contemptuously called 'cowardly women', dispersed his warriors. He could not account for his defeat at Wood Lake, even with the cannon, unless (he said) it was caused by traitors in his army.

For all of his brave talk, Little Crow had lost his will to fight and was on the run for Dakota Territory with other chiefs. There he holed up at Devil's Lake. The old villain wanted to torture all captives to death, in revenge for his defeat at Wood Lake. Chief Red Iron successfully argued against this sordid action. However, Indians guarding the makeshift prison camp raped some of the women captives.

(Contrary to frontier belief, this was not the inevitable consequence of Indian captivity.) Still, the Santees released 400 prisoners only three days after the battle. Within a month or so, 2000 Sioux surrendered.

The Minnesota Uprising took the lives of about 700 whites at a time when the North was used to casualty figures in the thousands. But the Civil War did not harden the nation to the horrors of senseless torture and murder of housewives and little girls and ribbon clerks and farm hands by these barbaric 'wards' of the government. Americans everywhere were shocked. Minnesotans developed a burning hatred for Indians and a demand for prompt vengeance. This hatred stoked fiery reprisals by militiamen on campaigns and led to a mass execution that is unique in the Indian Wars and, in fact, in all American history.

Sibley selected the 400 most guilty Indians to clap in irons and another 60 or 70 to place under close surveillance. The military commission that he set up sentenced 303 men to be hanged. Sibley sent the names to the President for confirmation.

In some areas of the country, sympathy still remained with the Indians, in spite of their atrocities, because of the many wrongs done them, for years, by whites. Abraham Lincoln was convinced that inflamed passions were trying to make a right out of two wrongs in Minnesota. He appointed two commissioners to review the evidence and determine, objectively, the various degrees of guilt of the Sioux charged with war crimes.

The Indians were marched first to a stockade at Fort Snelling and then to one on the Mankato River. Settlers lined the roads to turn them into gauntlets, striking at the passing Indians with stones, clubs, even garden hoes. They injured 15 of the prisoners and snatched one infant from its mother's arms and dashed it to death on the ground.

There was confusion over Sioux names and identities. The worst culprits were in hiding in Dakota Territory or Canada. No wonder that Lincoln set aside all but 38 sentences.

On the day after Christmas, 1862, the 38 condemned Sioux in Mankato were made to stand in four rows around the edge of a platform with nooses fitted around their necks and hoods over their heads. Ingeniously, the cutting of a single rope sprang all of the gallows trapdoors at once. Hangman William Duley (Dooley?) enjoyed his grim task. He had seen the Santees kill and scalp two of his children. The bodies were dumped in a mass grave but, in a final act of ignominy, they were disinterred by ghouls for laboratory experiments.

Little Crow, after trying without success to secure British support at Fort Garry (Winnipeg), foolishly returned to his old haunts with a few followers in the summer of 1863 to raid settlers in McLeod and Meeker Counties. On 3 July a settler killed him when he caught him on his farm picking raspberries. His scalp, taken as a trophy, was given to the Minnesota Historical Society. But his body was not buried, just left in the field as offal.

The Teton Sioux Battles

Among the insurrectionists who fled westward were the four young murderers who caused the awful war. They poured out their hatred of whites amongst the Teton Sioux of Dakota Territory and their Cheyenne and Arapaho friends.

Sibley, made a brigadier general in thanks for the Wood Lake victory, made expeditions into the Dakotas in the summers of 1863 and 1864 with 3000 men. He engaged in several skirmishes but it was General Alfred Sully, son of the famous painter, Thomas Sully, who hurt the Sioux. He was too late to link up with Sibley, but campaigned westward from Devil's Lake to the Yellowstone River with Iowa, Nebraska and Dakota citizen-soldiers.

At Whitestone Hill, North Dakota, on 3 September 1863, Sully slammed into a huge force of Sioux, 4000 people, of whom a thousand were warriors. The chief was Inkpaduta, who had carried out the Spirit Lake Massacre of 1857, a preview of the Santee uprising. (Ironically, Little Crow had helped the whites against Inkpaduta in 1857.) The battle was a catastrophe for the Sioux; they lost 300 braves and had 250 children and women captured at a cost to Sully of 22 dead and 50 wounded. After establishing Fort Rice on the upper Missouri to restrain the Tetons 'infected' by fleeing Santees, Sully took 2200 men against the Sioux again at **Kildeer Mountain**. He lost only five killed and ten wounded, and the Indians admitted a loss of 35. (Sully figured that their losses were closer to 100 or even 150.) The main thing was that they fled in the night, leaving all of their provisions. Sully said, 'I would rather destroy their supplies than kill 50 of their warriors'. The Teton Sioux were far from crushed, but they were whipped by Sully into an inclination for (temporary) peace.

The Yankton Sioux tended their crops on the Crow Creek Reservation; the Santees were confined by 1857 treaties to the Sisseton, Santee and Devil's Lake Reservations.

Kit Carson and the Navajo and Apache Battles

General James Carleton's choice of an officer to put a stop to nuisance raids by Mescalero Apaches and Navajos was an excellent one. Colonel Christopher (Kit) Carson was a plainsman, scout and ex-Rocky Mountain fur trader. An Indian agent from 1853 to 1861, he resigned in order to fight Confederates (and did so at the Battle of Valverde in February, 1862), not to combat Indians with whom he was likely to be in sympathy. But the illiterate colonel of New Mexico Volunteers was always in awe of successful, lettered, doers like John C Fremont and Carleton, and he allowed himself to be talked into heading a campaign against the Mescaleros.

Carleton wanted no talks with these Apaches. Women and children were to be taken prisoners, but all men were to be killed. The easy-going Carson discounted this showy ruthlessness of the General's.

Kit reoccupied Fort Stanton in southeast New Mexico and campaigned from there. After Lieutenant William Graydon outfought a war party, killing its two chiefs and nine warriors, the Mescalero Apaches began to sue for peace. They were pretty fair fighters. They carried in their left hands, or slung around their necks when not in action, shields which were of the size, shape and toughness of barrelheads. They were impervious to most pistol balls even at close range, beyond ten paces, and impenetrable at any real distance by glancing shots from muskets. But the Mescaleros did not have their hearts in the war. Soon, Carson was driving 400 of them to Bosque Redondo.

Bosque Redondo Reservation, a round grove of cottonwoods on the bank of the Pecos River under the guns of Fort Sumner, was called by the General's numerous critics, with tongues firmly in cheeks, 'Fair Carletonia'. It was a bleak and alkaline flat, dreary in the extreme.

Carson's campaign pretty well ended the Mescalero menace, though some young ones continued to raid from the safety of the Bosque Redondo Reservation. Kit tried to resign his colonelcy, to return to his family in Taos, but Carleton would not hear of it. He wanted him to repeat his success with the *Diné*, or Navajos.

Hostilities with the Navajos

Less truculent than their Apache kin, the Navajos, nevertheless, had lived a life of raiding livestock and enslaving women and children from both Mexicans and Pueblo Indians. (Naturally, both of the latter retaliated by enslaving Navajo youngsters.) General Alexander Doniphan had made peace with the Navajos during the Mexican War but expeditions into *Dinetah*, or Navajo Land, were necessary throughout the 1850s. At one point, the Navajos even besieged Fort Defiance itself.

Carleton thought that Bosque Redondo was just the place for the Navajos and that tough, patient, self-reliant Carson was just the man to put them there.

The tribal leadership was split into factions. Barboncito and Delgadito were, more or less, for peace. Manuelito was aloof, almost hostile. There was even a split-off group allied closely with the Army as scouts against their own people, called The Enemy Navajos by the *Diné*.

But all Navajos, from Manuelito to wee children, were possessed of a remarkably intense, even devout, love for their homeland. They refused to consider for even a moment the proposal that they migrate 300 miles from such sacred places as Cañón de Chelly to the barren Pecos flats, where the whites intended to turn them from semi-nomads into civilized, Christianized, self-sufficient farmers.

Any hope of cooperation by Navajos was ended in September 1861 when Lieutenant Colonel J F Chávez, commanding Fort Fauntleroy (Fort Lyon), let a contested horse race between New Mexicans and Navajos deteriorate into a riot, and then a small massacre. *Anglo* soldiers were prevented by *Hispano* officers from protecting the Indians. Chávez even ordered his howitzers to open fire on the men, women and children as they fled the fort. Sergeant Nicholas Hodt pretended that he did not hear the order. Still, a dozen people were killed and, the Navajos said, 112 were enslaved. General Canby rebuked Chávez, but his announced court-martial never took place.

The publicly-unbending Carleton issued an ultimatum to the unyielding Navajos on 23 June 1863. The Indians had till 27 July to come in peacefully for transfer to Bosque Redondo. After that, said the General, 'Every Navajo that is seen will be considered as hostile and treated accordingly.'

Carson was given 736 men to tackle the Navajos, described as vexatious, insidious, perfidious folk, no more to be trusted than the wolves of the mountains. Besides infantry and cavalry, Kit had Apache and Ute scouts. He had a few good officers such as Captains Asa B Carey and Albert H Pfeiffer and a number of absolutely useless drunkards and worse.

Pfeiffer, a former Ute and Apache Indian agent, joined the column late. Some New Mexicans considered him to be 'the most desperately courageous and successful Indian

fighter in the West'. He was an Indian-hater after June 1863. Apaches caught him while bathing in a hot spring on the Jornada del Muerto, slaughtered his wife and her servant, and chased him, naked, back to Fort McRae. He was himself wounded in the side by an arrow.

Carson halted his tired animals at Ojo del Oso (Bear Spring), site of Fort Fauntleroy-Lyon, and began a scorched earth policy by turning his animals into the Navajos' wheat fields. He also lived off the land, taking corn and 75,000 pounds of wheat from the Navajo fields at Pueblo Colorado Wash, near Ganado. At abandoned Fort Defiance in Cañón Bonito south of Chinle Wash and mysterious Cañón de Chelly, he again turned Indian croplands into pasture for his mounts. Kit built Fort Canby near the ruins of old Fort Defiance.

By now, Carson was tired of his incompetent officers. He forced the resignation of an alcoholic major after that hero bragged of being the best pimp in all New Mexico. Next, he forced a lieutenant to resign after he was found drunk and in bed with an enlisted man, while officer of the day. One of Kit's surgeons was a drunk, too. A vindictive major who seized Navajos and tried to humiliate them into 'escaping', so that he could invoke the old Spanish *ley de fuga* and kill them, had to be relieved of duty, also. Another lieutenant was caught, 'beastly intoxicated' and in bed with a friend, but at least it was a woman and not an enlisted man. Another lieutenant filed a false report about imaginary Navajo casualties and was forced to resign.

Above: **Colonel Christopher (Kit) Carson** was a trapper and fur trader in the 1830s, a scout for John C Frémont in the 1840s and the Ute Indian Agent in the 1850s. In the 1860s General James Carleton chose Carson to head a campaign to fight the Mescaleros and Navajos. Carson succeeded in driving the Mescaleros to Basque Redondo in exile. In 1864 his attack on the Comanches at Adobe Walls achieved only a draw.

Above: The Ruins of **White House**, a multi-storied cliff dwelling, is one of several that bear silent testimony to the level of culture attained by the pre-Columbian Anasasi people who populated Cañón de Chelly.

Right: **Cañón de Chelly**, with its high walls, was a natural fortress in the nineteenth century. Today it is populated only by a handful of Navajos and is accessible only by four-wheel-drive vehicles.

Below: The life-style of the **Navajos** in Cañón de Chelly today is little changed from that of their grandfathers, who encountered Kit Carson here.

Above: In his painting *After the Skirmish* Frederick Remington depicts the cavalrymen relaxing in the dusty heat of the Southwest.

Opposite page: Cañón de Chelly, near the New Mexican border in Arizona, was peaceful when George Wheeler's expedition explored it in the 1870s. In 1864 Carson was assigned to crush the Navajos and he turned the Navajos stronghold-sanctuary into a battleground. The 8000 Navajos surrendered and were also marched into exile to Basque Redondo.

The Navajos killed Major Joseph Cummings while he was on a scout, but there were few casualties on either side, even with Kit's relentless Navajo-haters, the Ute scouts. Only a few warriors were killed, though some women and children were captured and much property destroyed in Carson's search-and-destroy missions. He confiscated or killed all ponies he found, destroyed all corn and wheat fields and chopped down some of the Navajos' prized peach trees. But he was not severe with the Navajo *people*; he wanted them prisoners, not dead.

Delgadito gave up in this war of attrition in November 1863 but Carson had less than 200 Navajos to forward to Bosque Redondo. The turning point came with Carson's invasion in January 1864 of the tribe's inner sanctum, **Canón de Chelly**. Army units had scouted it before, but it was still largely unknown territory to the Army. It was a sanctuary to the *Diné*, the site of their last-ditch stand.

Carson held the mouth of the Cañón and sent Pfeiffer to scour it from the eastern head. By mistake, he descended into the tributary Cañón del Muerto after a taxing march in the snow. Navajos dropped boulders on his men from the rims high above, but he flushed all warriors from the defile and followed it to its intersection with the main Cañón de Chelly. The Navajos, caught between Carson and Pfeiffer, began to give up. They were cold, hungry and afraid to build fires which would give their positions away.

By the summer of 1864, Carson accepted the largest Indian surrender in history. By year's end, 8000 people were marched from Forts Defiance and Wingate to exile at Bosque Redondo. Carey, not Carson, supervised this Southwestern version of the Cherokee Trail of Tears. The less poetic Navajos called the bitter experience The Long Walk. Many people died on the long march even though the soldiers, taking their cues from Carson and Carey, pitied their charges more than they hated them. Some went on half-rations to share their food. The Navajos were disarmed for the march, but their guns were returned to them at Bosque Redondo. About 4000 Navajos under Manuelito held out in the West, but surrendered in 1866.

Kit allowed himself to be talked into supervising Bosque Redondo, but gave it up as hopeless after only a few months. The Navajos were not ill-treated at the agency, except by some Mescaleros, but it was a wretched place and they were desperately homesick and unhappy. Their headmen continued to beg to be returned to the New Mexico-Arizona country. General Sherman, shocked at the conditions at Bosque Redondo, approved the move *if* the Navajos promised to remain peaceful. Otherwise, he swore, they would be sent to Oklahoma Indian Territory. In 1868 the Indian Bureau relented and allowed the Navajos to return to their land. Carleton's experiment was a failure but the Navajos never went back on their word, expressed in the 1868 treaty. They never went on the warpath again.

Attack on the Cheyenne

By 1864 the Arapahos and Cheyennes of Colorado were almost as starved as the Navajos pinned atop Cañón de Chelly's Fortress Rock. Hunger sent them raiding the South Platte trails. But hunger was no excuse for the campaign of scalping and mutilating of victims and the burning of their homesteads. After supplies and mail were cut off from Denver and stages stopped running, authorities in that town inflamed public opinion by putting on exhibit the scalped and otherwise abused corpses of a settler, his wife and their two children.

The time was ripe for a hero to save Colorado from what its settlers, without blinking, called savagery. Major Jacob Downing surprised a Cheyenne encampment at Cedar Bluffs, a canyon 90 miles north of the South Platte. He gave the order, 'Commence killing!' and at the cost of one

Above: A photograph of **Ouray**, the chief of the Uncompahgre Utes.

Opposite page: **Manuelito**, the last Indian chief to surrender (1866) in the Navajo War, held out with his 4000 followers long after Kit Carson moved most of his people to Bosque Redondo on the Pecos River in Texas. He was photographed when he was in Washington, DC, with a *Dineh* delegation.

man dead and another wounded, wiped out 26 Indians and wounded perhaps 60 more, who got away. Downing boasted, 'I took no prisoners'. He said that only a shortage of ammunition prevented him from hunting down and killing more Cheyennes.

But Downing was not the man of the hour. That honor went to the hero of the Battle of Glorieta Pass, the man whose audacity turned the battle around and sent the Texans fleeing from the Far Southwest on 27 March 1862. Colonel John M Chivington was called 'The Fighting Parson' because he was a minister who had spurned a chaplaincy, a 'praying commission', in order to fight Rebels and Redskins.

In November of 1864 Chivington made it known that he was going to attack Black Kettle's Cheyennes. Brother officers argued that that particular band had surrendered already and was under the protection of Major Edward Wynkoop of Fort Lyon. But the ineffable 'man of God' just retorted that it was his belief that it was right and honorable to use any means under God's heaven to exterminate the people he characterized as 'women and children-killing savages'. And he added, 'Damn any man who is in sympathy with Indians!'

Black Kettle, camped on **Sand Creek**, an Arkansas River tributary, was probably an ambiguous fellow. He may have murdered settlers, but, at the moment, he was choosing the course of peace. A careful man, he had both a white flag and

a Stars and Stripes to fly over his lodge to indicate his peaceable nature.

If Chivington actually saw the flags, he probably suspected treachery. Whatever the case, he fell on the unsuspecting village with 700 men and four howitzers. He separated the warriors from their pony herd as Black Kettle tried to reassure his people that they would not be killed. Soon, the chief had to flee with his wounded wife behind him on his horse. Perhaps remembering the grisly display in Denver, Chivington's men offered no quarter to anyone. The brutalized soldiers scalped and mutilated the dead. Chivington ran the Cheyennes for five miles, on a trail littered with corpses, giving up the chase only when darkness closed in.

Sand Creek was a battle, but it was a massacre also. The bloody parson had seven men killed outright and 47 wounded, of whom seven more died. But only two women and five children were taken prisoners. (Chivington wanted no prisoners.) And one report had a body count of the Indian dead totaling only 26 warriors of between 200 and 400 (estimates differed) dead on the field.

The 'Bloody 3rd' paraded in downtown Denver in triumph and a theater exhibited 100 Indian scalps on its stage. But the general public, to Chivington's surprise, was outraged by Sand Creek. After all, a witness had seen a three year-old shot by a soldier. Interpreter John Smith reported women ripped open with knives, children clubbed to death and then mutilated.

A congressional invesigation issued 700 pages of testimony and condemned Chivington's actions. The embittered colonel was called to appear before a court-martial but was allowed to resign his commission without being punished. For years, the country was split into two camps by the shock of Sand Creek.

Battle of Adobe Walls

Chivington's opposite, Kit Carson, had one more campaign to carry out during the Civil War in the West. He rode out of Fort Bascom, New Mexico, in November with a force of New Mexican and Californian Volunteers and Ute auxiliaries. He was after hostile Kiowas, Cheyennes and Comanches. At **Adobe Walls**, the melting remnants of William Bent's old trading post in the Canadian River Valley of the Texas Panhandle, Carson fell on a combined force of Comanches and Kiowas which outnumbered him two to one. Victory was uncertain until Kit unlimbered his pair of 12-pound mountain howitzers. 'Throw a few shells into that crowd over there', was typical of his unmilitary commands. As fresh warriors sought to encircle him under the cover of smoke from a grass fire that they had set, Carson used a smokescreen of his own.

This First Battle of Adobe Walls was claimed by Kit as a victory, mainly because he was able to burn all 150 Kiowa lodges with all of their winter stores. But it was more like a draw, even with the artillery. Carson lost two killed and had ten wounded, and probably exaggerated a bit in guessing that his men killed 60 Kiowas and Comanches.

Carson's Battle of Adobe Walls took place on 25 November 1864. Just 19 weeks later, 9 April 1865. General Robert E Lee surrendered the Confederate Army to General Ulysses S Grant at Appomattox Court House. An era ended, but a new one would begin in the Indian Wars of the West.

BEHIND EVERY BUSH: ESCALATION OF HOSTILITIES IN THE LATE 1860s

There would be more than 200 fights in the West during the decade that followed the Civil War. New outposts and improved weaponry, combined with the strengthening of existing garrisons, brought renewed vigor into the fighting. The post-Civil War era saw mobile cavalry troops replacing slower infantry companies, and skirmishes exploded into two series of wars that were to dominate the West for a long time to come, especially in the North Plains and in the Southwest.

July 1865 brought the first major conflict between Indians and whites after the Civil War had ended. The Sioux, Cheyenne and Arapaho had been plotting a great campaign against the whites since May. The place they began was near Casper, Wyoming, named for Lieutenant Casper W Collins, who was a transient officer unlucky enough to be stuck at the Platte River Bridge Station at the wrong time. Some 200 miles west of Fort Laramie lay not just an improved river crossing, a ford, but a bona fide span where the California-Oregon Trail crossed the North Platte. Near the bridge a tiny village sprang up—a store, a stage station, and a stockaded fort sometimes called Camp Dodge.

Unknown to Collins or his commanding officer, Major Martin Anderson, 3000 Sioux, Arapaho and Cheyenne were hiding in the sandstone bluffs near the stockade, trying to decide how and when to attack.

First, the lurking Indians tried to draw the soldiers out by sending a few decoys across the flat in front of the fort. But the Army, secure behind its log walls, would not budge, only responding with desultory howitzer fire. When reinforcements rode up, the Indians attacked them, but they got safely into the fort under covering fire from its walls.

On the morning of 26 July the besiegers tried to draw their noose tighter. They placed men both above and below the bridge to isolate it. They sent decoys even closer, to canter across the prairie in plain view of the sentries.

Opposite page: Charles M Bell's 1880 photo is a portrait of **Red Cloud**, or **Scarlet Cloud (Makhpiya Luta)** c. 1822-1909, the Oglala Sioux who set back Army plans for the Bozeman Trail for years.

This time it appeared that the Army was swallowing the bait. The gates opened and a cavalry detachment trotted across the Platte Bridge. They were not chasing Indian decoys, but going out to escort an approaching supply train, spotted in the distance by a sentry on a wall. A round was fired from a howitzer to warn the train's escort of possible trouble.

Collins was in command of the 20 Kansas troopers only because none of their officers wanted to risk their lives so close to demobilization. The lieutenant was apprehensive. It is said that his fear of death lead him to wear his brand-new dress uniform on the mission.

Two long columns of Indians now made their moves. One rode out of a brushy draw and passed behind Collins, cutting him off from the bridge. The other moved in front of him, separating him from the five wagons guarded by Sergeant Amos J Custard and 25 men.

Collins spurred his unit forward to break the forming circle and, at the same time, to relieve the wagons. His men loosed a volley with their carbines, slid them back into their scabbards and broke out six-shooters. But the firing in his rear led Collins to order a retreat to the bridgehead. He led the way, slashing with his saber in head-to-head combat, troopers and Indians intermingled. The pistols took their toll at such close quarters, but when Collins turned back to pick up a wounded man, he was killed. Four of his men were also killed and eight more seriously wounded. All of the rest were hurt, too, but the wounded got back to the fort.

Custard, seeing his rescue party battered into a retreat, drew his wagons into the age-old circular posture of defense. It was the Sergeant's misfortune that he drew as an opponent a real fighter. Like Custard, he was only a warrior, not a chief. But he had many followers because of his fighting prowess. He was huge, 230-pound Roman Nose, a giant among Indians at six feet three inches in height. He thought himself well nigh invincible in battle, too, because of the strong medicine of his war bonnet.

The Cheyenne did not choose to have his men circle the trapped train on horseback, to be picked off by the con-

Below: In 1919, Charles M Russell painted this oil on canvas, *The Buffalo Hunt*, now in the Amon Carter Museum. He showed the manner in which Plains Indians, mounted on nimble-footed ponies, circled a milling bison herd for close-range shots with bows and arrows and rifles they acquired from the whites.

cealed riflemen. He dismounted half of his braves and they crawled up on their bellies toward the wagonmen. The other half kept the fort busy. There would be no help for Custard from that quarter.

With astounding patience, Roman Nose settled down and took four hours to capture the wagons, killing and mutilating everybody and burning to death the last survivors, including the wounded sergeant. He might have taken the fort, too, but the Indians were unused to long sieges and had been badly hurt by Collins and Custard—suffering up to 60 dead and 130 wounded—so they broke off the attack and withdrew.

General Connor's Expedition of 1865

While the Indians were making scattered raids, such as that at Platte Bridge, the Army was concentrating on only one thing. The Californian, General Patrick Edward Connor, was trying to mount a major offensive, one worthy of the Civil War campaigns in the East. But the **Powder River Expedition** was slowed by muddy terrain, bad weather, mutinous troops, short rations and inadequate forage for the animals. Volunteers demanded their discharges. And some got them. Alarms from the Black Hills and Minnesota siphoned off Connor's manpower.

Finally, Connor moved out three columns to rendezvous at Rosebud Creek around 1 September 1865. Colonel Nelson Coe took the Right Column of 1400 men and Lieutenant Colonel Samuel Walker the Center Column of 600-plus men—but only after Connor faced the rebellious Kansans with his Californians and a loaded howitzer. Connor himself took the Left Column, about 600 men including Captain Frank North's Pawnee Scouts, with Jim Bridger as guide. It was the biggest Army operation in the West, except perhaps for the combined Sibley-Sully punitive raids of the Santee War.

Connor had several skirmishes, in one of which his Pawnees bested a Cheyenne war party. Near the Bozeman Trail crossing of Powder River he built Fort Connor, then fought a bloody draw with Black Bear's Arapahos. Red Cloud's Oglala Sioux and Dull Knife's Cheyennes were harassing his two other units, but he did not know it.

It was now 11 September and the only information on Cole and Walker that Connor had was the discovery by his Pawnees of hundreds of their horses, dead, and their saddles burned. Finally, with the Pawnees' help, the link-up was made on 24 September. But two of the three divisions of the Powder River Expedition were complete wrecks. Both Cole and Walker happened to cover ground which was without water or grass. Their horses died and their men were put on short rations. Cole's men escaped disaster by using their cannon, especially a rifled piece, and their Spencer repeaters effectively. But a sleeting norther crippled the now-combined force. Most horses were dead and most men starving when Connor rescued them.

Luckily for Connor, new orders arrived to break up the too-vast District of the Plains into four manageable districts. It was with relief that he terminated the expedition and headed for Salt Lake City.

The real reason for the Army's discontinuance of Connor's campaign was its excessive cost. The Army hurriedly cut back on large-scale operations. The Quartermaster General himself went west to investigate the expenditure in the District of ten millions for rations and forage and an

equal sum for other supplies. The Indians were bankrupting the Army!

The great expedition of 1865 was a failure, though not the ignominious defeat that it has sometimes been painted. It was true that Cole and Walker barely avoided a disaster. And while the former claimed to have killed or wounded from 200 to 500 Indians, the latter confessed that his men might not have killed a single warrior. But Connor fought the Arapahos to a bloody draw and his Pawnees won a skirmish. Connor was a good man, but the combination of hostiles, bad terrain and filthy weather beat his unwieldy army. Worst of all, his supposedly powerful expedition, instead of chastening the Indians, only emboldened them.

Failed Diplomacy at Fort Laramie

Before the Army replaced Volunteers with battle-hardened Civil War veterans from an Army reduced to only 25,000 enlisted men, the Government tried to duplicate Fitzpatrick's diplomacy of 1851. Another great Fort Laramie pow-wow was held on 13–16 June 1866 although General John Pope warned that the Indians meant to fight,

that they considered their treaties to be just white men's scraps of paper. In the chair was no less a personage than the Civil War hero, General William T ('War is Hell') Sherman, now commanding the District of the Plains which was being carved up into separate commands.

Sherman enticed Red Cloud, Dull Knife, Spotted Tail and other chiefs with goodwill gifts of powder, lead and food. Although they had turned back Connor, the Indians had been punished by the hard winter almost as much as the Expedition had suffered.

The Government asked permission for emigrants to cross the lands recently granted to the Sioux and Cheyenne, but the General also sought permission for three forts to be built on the Bozeman Trail connecting the Platte River with Montana's mines. Sherman knew that the chiefs were not Roman dictators; they could not guarantee, in advance, the conduct of their young warriors.

Red Cloud of the Oglalas spoke for both the Sioux and Cheyennes though he was, technically, not a chief. A born leader, he adamantly opposed any such concessions. He angrily broke off the talks when he saw Colonel Henry B Carrington's 700 men of the 18th Infantry marching through Fort Laramie on their way to build the forts in the Powder River country regardless of the council's outcome. When Carrington entered the peace tent, Red Cloud jumped to his feet and (correctly) accused the leaders in Washington of deceit, sending presents to buy a road while sending 'eagles'—he pointed to Carrington's symbols of rank—to steal it. He added, 'I prefer to die fighting rather than by starvation.'

All of the chiefs muttered their disgust at the Government's bald deception. Man Afraid of His Horses warned Sherman that his people would resist both road and forts. Almost all of the chiefs left in a huff, though three Brulés

Below left: The **Spotted Tail** Agency, later the Rosebud Agency, abutted the Oglalas on the west. The Brule chief was more peaceful than Red Cloud and his agency more peaceable until he was killed by Crow Dog in 1881. Out of anarchy emerged the Ghost Dance.

Below: At a second Fort Laramie great peace-making pow-wow, held in 1868, the Army faced the Indian delegates with an impressive array of general officers including (together, right of center pole) **William S Harney** and **William T Sherman** and, behind the bush, **Alfred Terry**.

signed. Later, however, even they notified Sherman that their braves had repudiated their action. They warned all whites to look out for their scalps.

Colonel Carrington did not make policy, of course. He just carried out orders. But he was lumped by Chief Spotted Tail with the bureaucrats, all being liars in the chief's opinion. But Carrington was, at least, wise enough to resist a splendid example of penny-wise, pound-foolish Washington policy making. When orders came to fire his scout, mountain man Jim Bridger, to save his five dollars a day in pay, Carrington lied that the discharge was 'impossible to execute.'

As it was, the Government seemed hellbent on sending him into disaster with only a couple of howitzers and 700 men armed, mostly, with obsolete muzzle-loading Springfield rifled muskets. Only his bandsmen had seven-shot Spencer carbines.

Colonel Carrington's Campaign

After Sherman's pow-wow fell apart, Carrington proceeded west from Laramie with his long line of 226 wagons. They bore not only the usual lead, powder and rations, but also doors, window sills, locks, chains, butter churns, musical instruments, seeds for vegetable gardens, scythes and mowing machines, tools, blacksmith's forges, shingle and brick-making machines, even a steam-powered sawmill. Apparently the Army meant to stay in the Powder River-Bighorn country; in the rear were ambulances or light wagons with Army wives and children.

At Fort Reno, old Fort Connor, 175 miles from Fort Laramie, Carrington on 28 June 1866 relieved Galvanized Yankee Confederates and Michigan Volunteers with his regulars. Some of his men he sent on reconnaissances, using the Volunteers' horses. He left a quarter of his men at Fort Reno and moved the balance to a grassy flat between the forks of (Big) Piney and Little Piney Creeks near the Powder River. It was a superb site, with lots of grass, water and even nearby timber.

Carrington was a good man for the job of fort-building. A Yale graduate, he was both a draftsman and an engineer. But the Sioux slowed construction of his powerful 600-by-800 foot stockade of Fort Phil Kearny by picking off sentries on knolls and shooting up haying and woodcutting fatigue parties until frightened off by a few howitzer rounds. They then returned at night to snipe at sentries on the fort's rising walls. Worst of all was the gauntlet that had to be run by the wood wagons, seven miles from fort to timber.

It dawned on Carrington that he was being held a virtual prisoner in his new fort, so he appealed for more men and ammunition. He got 95 infantrymen and 65 cavalry recruits so green that the latter could hardly sit a horse. The position of the Government, which knew best, of course, was that the Powder River area was at peace.

All the while, Red Cloud and Dull Knife were being joined by allies: Black Bear of the Arapahos, Sitting Bull and Gall of the Hunkpapa Sioux, the bright young Oglala Sioux warrior, Crazy Horse, and the Miniconjou, Hump. Even some of peaceful Spotted Tail's men joined the loose siege of the three forts, Carrington having added Fort C F Smith on the Bighorn River.

Jim Bridger arranged a talk between Carrington and Red Cloud. The former tried both to please the latter with band music and to scare him with demonstrations of howitzer fire. It did not work. The very next morning Red Cloud ran off 175 of the Colonel's horses and mules. When Army pursuers were well strung out, the Indians turned on them. So, casually, began the bloody Red Cloud's War.

Red Cloud was serious, *deadly* serious. Old Gabe Bridger learned that he had even tried to get his deadly enemies, the Crows, to join the great war against the whites. In this he failed, but he got some modern weapons from the Sioux who lazed about Fort Laramie. This was important, for most of his braves still had only bows and arrows. Now Crazy Horse became an expert at decoying cavalrymen into traps.

Carrington made a brave show of formally celebrating the completion of the key fort of the three, Phil Kearny, by raising the Stars and Stripes on the last day of October, then hosting a feast and quadrille after a speech by himself. But there was really little cause for celebration. Morale was low, because he had not drilled or trained his troopers, but had used them as workmen. The strongly-built fort was understrength to act as the cutting edge of the frontier. Figuratively speaking, Fort Phil Kearny was cantilevered out over an abyss.

The Fetterman Massacre

Jim Bridger continued to warn Carrington that Indian trouble, bad trouble, was brewing. Cocky younger officers, veterans of Sherman's fiery march to the sea in the Civil War, mocked him and derided Carrington's obsession with defense. Captain Frederick H Brown even delayed a transfer back East in order to get a crack at the Indians. He boasted that he would, personally, lift Red Cloud's scalp. He was outdone in braggadocio by Captain William J Fetterman, who bragged that he would march through the entire Sioux nation if given just 80 good troopers.

On 6 December Red Cloud baited Carrington and Fetterman with a fake raid on a wood train and stung them badly. By 21 December he was ready for the main event. He hid between 1500 and 2000 warriors behind Lodge Trail Ridge and laid an ambush on Peno Creek, only three miles from the fort. Crazy Horse and Hump led two small parties of decoys close to the fort as another band struck at the wood train. The pickets on the walls of Fort Phil Kearny, as usual, fired warning shots. Carrington promptly ordered out Captain James Powell to escort the woodcutters to safety.

But Fetterman wanted his taste of glory. He demanded the command on the basis of his brevet seniority, and he got it. Carrington gave him clear and strict orders. He was to go to the aid of the wood train only. He was not to pursue the raiders beyond Lodge Trail Ridge under any conditions.

Privately, of course, Fetterman considered Carrington much too cautious for his own good. He selected two firebrands, Brown and Lieutenant George W Grummond. The latter had almost been killed in a skirmish but had, seemingly, learned nothing. He left behind in the fort his bride of only a few months.

The overconfidence of these brash officers should have shocked the cautious Carrington into replacing them or revoking his orders. But he could not. His thoughts were on the safety of the trapped wood-cutting crew. As if it were a picnic, or a hunt, two civilians casually joined the detachment just to try out (on live targets) their new rapid fire Henry repeating rifles.

Major Battles in The West
(1857-1875)

BRITISH COLUMBIA

NORTHWEST TERRITORIES

ONTARIO

WASHINGTON TERRITORY

Portland
Ft Walla Walla
Ft Missoula

MONTANA TERRITORY
Ft Benton
Helena
Butte

Ft Union
DAKOTA
MINNESOTA
Kildeer Mtn (1864)
Big Mound (1863)
Ft Abraham Lincoln

OREGON TERRITORY
Rogue River Wars (1851-56)

Ft Keogh
Ft Custer

Whitestone Hill (1863)

WISCONSIN
Minneapolis
St Paul

IDAHO TERRITORY
Ft Bridger

Hayfield (1867)
Tongue (1865)
Fetterman (1866)
Wagon Box (1867)
Ft Phil Kearney
Crazy Woman (1866)

TERRITORY
Ft Pierre
Deadwood
Sawyer Expedition Ambush (1865)

Wood Lake (1862)
Birch Coulee (1862)
New Ulm

IOWA

Battle Mountain (1861)

Ft Fetterman

WYOMING TERRITORY
Ft Laramie

NEBRASKA TERRITORY
Cheyenne

Spirit Lake (1857)

Omaha

Chicago (Missouri Military Division HQ)

Sacramento
Reno
San Francisco (Pacific Military Division HQ)

Salt Lake City

NEVADA TERRITORY

UTAH TERRITORY
Mountain Meadows Massacre (1857)

Leadville
Denver
Cripple Creek
Sand Creek Massacre (1864)

Missouri
Ft Kearny

ILLINOI

Massacre Canyon (1873)
Beecher Island (1868)

Ft Leavenworth
Ft Riley

River

Independence
St. Louis

CALIFORNIA

Canyon de Chelly (1864)
Ft Defiance

COLORADO TERRITORY

KANSAS
MISSOURI

ARIZONA

Taos
Ft Union
Santa Fe

Ft Supply
OKLA
INDIAN

Ft Apache

Adobe Walls (1864 & 1874)
Washita (1868)
Tule & Palo Duro Canyons (1874)
Okmulgee

ARKANSAS

Ft Yuma

Salt River Canyon (1872)
STAKED PLAINS
Ft Sill
TERRITORY

Tucson

NEW MEXICO TERRITORY

Ft Worth Dallas

El Paso

MEXICO

TEXAS

San Antonio

LOUISIANA

Colorado River

● Cities
■ Forts
✗ Battles
　 Military Division of the Pacific
　 Military Division of the Missouri

Fetterman fancied himself a strategist as well as an Indian fighter. He did not head directly for the embattled woodsmen, but curved around to the rear of the marauders both to force a fight and to cut off their retreat. He was damned if he would let the redskins cheat him of his moment in the sun. The Indians countered in their usual fashion, Crazy Horse disengaging a few decoys. Fetterman fell for the trap, lock, stock and barrel. Either forgetting or, more likely, ignoring Carrington's orders, he galloped his force over Lodge Trail Ridge and out of sight of the fort.

On the far slope, quietly awaiting him, were Red Cloud and his main force, concealed in gullies. Once Crazy Horse gave the signal, the Sioux, Cheyenne and Arapahos fell on the 81-man force.

It was cold on the slope which came to be called Massacre Hill. Men and mounts slipped on ice and snow which soon became red with blood. Fetterman's trapdoor Springfields were dependable; they almost never jammed. And they were accurate. But, at such close range, the detachment could not have survived had they all carried Henry or Spencer repeaters instead of the single-shot arm.

Grummond, in the lead, was shot early on. Within an hour, every man was either shot down or was a suicide. Both Fetterman and Brown apparently shot themselves so that they would not have to endure the tortures of the Indians. The latter hacked, butchered and disemboweled the bodies with devilish glee, enjoying their humiliation of the dead. They even killed a pet dog of one of the soldiers. The Army called it the **Fetterman Massacre** because the rash lieutenant lost every man of his command. The Indians called it the Battle of a Hundred Slain.

This was the Army's worst defeat, so far, in the West, and only the second engagement in its history in which there were no survivors. It is often forgotten that the foolish Fetterman fought well before being overwhelmed and blowing his own brains out. Some Indians even said that their total of dead and wounded was 200, but it is doubtful that Red Cloud lost the 60 dead claimed by the Army.

The Hayfield Fight

The men of the wood train, ignored by the Indians busy with their blood bath, made it safely into the fort. The sound of rifle fire beyond the ridge led Carrington to put together the strongest rescue force that he could. He took almost every able-bodied man. He left the fort and the women and children protected only by bandsmen, cooks, and prisoners he released from the guardhouse. It was a terrible risk, for Red Cloud could have destroyed Carrington's force and taken the post. But, inexplicably, he withdrew before Carrington's counter-attack.

When the Colonel pulled back, he expected the fort to be overrun. He planned to blow up the powder magazine and the women and children with it, to keep them out of the hands of the savages. But the weather saved Fort Phil Kearny. A blizzard dropped the temperature to 30 below. It was actually much colder outside the fort because of the wind chill factor. Even with fires, warm woolen clothing and blankets, Carrington had to change his guard details every half-hour to keep the sentinels from freezing. In their thin-skinned *tipis* the besieging Indians were not so flushed with victory that they did not huddle together, miserably, in shivering masses.

Trapped in the snowbound fort, Carrington asked the impossible. He wanted a volunteer to ride to Fort Laramie to get help. John (Portugee) Phillips, a veteran scout, stepped forward. The Colonel gave him his own horse to ride, a Kentucky bluegrass thoroughbred. He personally led the brave scout out through the gate and called into the swirling snowflakes behind him, 'May God help you!'

Portugee Phillips's desperate journey became a feat by which all horseback rides in the West have since been measured. Often, stiff and cold and frostbitten as he was under his layered clothing and buffalo robe, he had to dismount and lead—flounder—his horse through waist-high snow drifts. Wisely, he hid by day and traveled only by night.

Phillips reached tiny Fort Reno safely, but there was no aid to be spared there, not even a telegraph to alert Fort Laramie. So he rode on as a band of pursuers closed on him. From the summit of a hill, he held them off till dark-

ness came and he could give them the slip. At Horseshoe Station, he had the telegrapher wire Fort Laramie but, not trusting the wires, he rode on to deliver his message in person. It was lucky that he did; the telegraph message did not get through.

In classic dramatic fashion, the completely exhausted horse and rider staggered into the fort to interrupt a gala Christmas Eve ball. Phillips was hardly able to speak. He was nearly dead from exhaustion and exposure. But he got through, and Fort Laramie rushed the 1st Battalion of the 18th Infantry Regiment to Fort Phil Kearny before Red Cloud could mount his attack. The hostiles dispersed.

Naturally the Army had to save face. Not content with Fetterman, they made Carrington a scapegoat and relieved him of his command.

Much too late, the Army sent west the ammunition and supplies Carrington had requested. Single shot—but breech loading—Springfield rifles replaced the old muzzle-loaders. A few repeating carbines made their way to the forts. Red Cloud's strategy was to besiege the posts in the hope of stopping all traffic with them. It was his ill luck to have to do so in the face of improved Army weapons.

The Indians struck on 1 and 2 August at both Fort Phil Kearny and Fort C F Smith. Some 500 Cheyennes caught 30 civilian hay cutters and soldier-guards two miles from the latter post on 1 August. The soldiers, sheltered in a log corral, shot the first rush of men to pieces. Only one warrior made it to the barricade and he was shot dead. The Cheyennes set the grass afire, but the flames stopped 20 feet short of the logs, 'as though arrested by supernatural power', one of the defenders said. The smoke blew back on

Below: Winter campaigning, a trademark of the Indian-fighting Army was hard on the troopers, but even harder on the Indians, who were often hungry and freezing in their *tipis.*

Above: An Indian fights a cavalry trooper in **The Duel** by Charles Schreyvogel. *Right:* **The Wagon Box Fight** near Fort Phil Kearny, 2 August 1867. Here Captain Powell's riflemen held off six Sioux charges.

the Indians, who used it to retrieve their 20 dead or wounded warriors.

The Wagon Box Fight

Guarding the ax-wielders at Fort Phil Kearny the day after the **Hayfield Fight** was a company of the 27th Infantry. They were struck by the elite of the Lakota nation—Red Cloud, Crazy Horse and American Horse. Crazy Horse first stampeded the mules and the horse herd, then split the axemen from their escort. But the wood crew, dropping tools and picking up rifles, made it safely back to the fort. This was because the 1500 Indians were intent on another Fetterman butchery, with Captain Powell their chief victim this time.

But Powell was no Fetterman or Brown or Grummond. He had carefully forted up his men in a strongpoint prepared for just such a crisis. It was a miniature fort of 14 wagon beds out in the open with a good field of fire for his 31 soldiers and civilians. The wagon boxes had been left behind when the wood crew took their wheels and axles to haul logs. Powell filled the interstices between the boxes with logs and sandbags made of grain sacks. He even took the precaution of placing extra arms and ammunition inside the wagon bodies for emergencies.

The Indians had been stung badly in the six-hour Hayfield Fight, when a dozen civilians and 20 soldiers fought off odds of at least 20-to-one for six hours. **The Wagon Box Fight** was a replay of that engagement—and more.

Powell gave his best sharpshooters three repeating rifles each, probably 50 caliber Spencers, with other soldiers at their sides to reload the guns. The rest of his men used their breech loading or trapdoor Springfields very well. He had his men hold their fire until the war-whooping 500 redmen were a scant 50 yards away. The sudden and unrelenting rain of fire split the Indian charge into bits. Never had the Sioux taken such losses and so quickly. At close range, some rifle-balls passed through one victim to kill or wound a second man behind him. There

were none of the lulls in firing, the loading delays, on which the Indians counted.

The Sioux and their allies fled, leaving dead men and horses all around the improvised fort. Powell lost six dead and two wounded of his 32-man force. For once, white estimates of Indian losses were probably accurate—60 dead and 120 wounded. The Indians had rushed the defenders six separate times and Red Cloud's horse was shot from under him, perhaps by Powell himself.

The Hayfield and Wagon Box Fights was a classic battles in which a few badly outnumbered men held off overwhelming odds.

While the Indians were virtually closing the Bozeman Trail to travelers, to the south another big Army push, like Connors's, was carried out by General W S Hancock and his right-hand man, the rising young star of the cavalry arm of the service, Colonel George A Custer. 'Hancock the

Superb' of Civil War fame knew little of Indians and this 1867 campaign was Custer's first brush with redskins. So thinly spread were troops in so many far-flung posts on the plains that most had to remain strictly on the defensive, thereby intimidating hostile Indians not a whit. Ironically, Hayfield and Wagon Box battles gave the Indians more pause than **'Hancock's War'** of 1867. Its major accomplishment, Custer's destruction of Roman Nose's camp on Pawnee Fork, was 'disallowed' by the Government as illegal and Hancock was relieved.

In the fall of 1867 Sherman and other generals negotiated the Medicine Lodge Treaty in Kansas to create two large reservations in Indian Territory, one for Cheyennes and Arapahos and the other for Comanches, Kiowas and Kiowa-Apaches. Then in April 1868 the generals once more parleyed with Red Cloud and, to the consternation of the Army, virtually surrendered to him. They con-

ceded all of his demands and abandoned the Bozeman Trail and its three forts. A shock wave ran through the Army, which felt betrayed—after its bloody sacrifices—by higher-ups. Embittered troopers, marching out of the Powder River country, looked over their shoulders to see clouds of smoke as the Indians fired the forts. And what did Sherman get in exchange? Red Cloud's word to 'try' to keep his young men off the warpath.

The Bozeman Trail capitulation by the Army not only emboldened Red Cloud but also Tall Bull, the jingoist Cheyenne who opposed pro-peace Black Kettle. He was one of 500 Dog Soldiers, a Cheyenne guard of elite warriors. Roman Nose refused to sign the Medicine Lodge Treaty and the tall brave was not about to go on a reservation. Like Tall Bull, he would roam and hunt where he pleased.

THE WINTER CAMPAIGN, THE RISE OF CUSTER, AND THE APACHE WARS

When General Philip Sheridan, the Commanding Officer of the Army's Department of the West, made a tour of inspection in 1868, peace was firmly in the saddle. The Indians were to be persuaded, not forced, to go onto reservations. But Sheridan knew that a policy of weakness would never work. It was the 93 Army posts that kept the peace, such as it was, not appeasement.

The rank and file despised the Peace Commission's policies which, as they saw it, amounted to feeding the Indians in winter so that they could kill soldiers and civilians the next summer. Sheridan, at least, later got his old comrade, President Grant, to end the practice of making treaties with Indian 'nations' as if they were foreign governments. The tribesmen would be considered simply wards of the Government.

But Federal vacillation continued to plague soldiers and settlers alike. Guns and ammunition, promised to the Cheyennes by the Indian Bureau, did not arrive because Tall Bear raided the peaceful Kaw Indians. But when he threatened more trouble, the Government handed out arms on 9 August 1868 at Fort Larned, Kansas.

A separate party of Cheyennes, unaware of the deal, changed its mind and instead of raiding Pawnees, as planned, turned on whites along the Solomon and Saline Rivers, burning ranches, running off livestock, killing men and raping women. Peaceful Indians hurried south to safety as the Dog Soldiers and their ilk terrorized eastern Colorado and western Kansas.

Sheridan, Hancock's successor, thought that the cure for these hostilities would be a surprise winter campaign. But if he waited, all of western Kansas would be afire. So he adopted a plan of Major George A Forsyth for the fall. Forsyth had worked his way up from dragoon private to brevet brigadier general during the Civil War. He wanted the Army to operate Indian-style. He would use a strong scouting force to dog and harass war parties so that they could never rest. It was a brilliant idea, much too logical

Facing page: **The Battle of Beecher Island**, Colorado in 1868. Major Forsyth withstood the attacks of Sioux, Cheyenne and Arapaho.

for the Army generals. He would split the hostiles into small and weak groups which would have to fight, and die, or surrender in a guerrilla war of attrition. He was sure that the Sioux and their allies, if kept hungry, off-balance and bloodied, would be able to besiege no forts, raid no stage-coaches.

Sheridan's approval brought the first 50 'first-class, hardy, frontiersmen' of hundreds of volunteers. Forsyth wanted real scouts, plainsmen, so he, deliberately, did not draw from the ranks but signed up tough civilians who were eager to fight Indians for a dollar a day. Because of Army red tape, he had to enlist his fighting men in the Quarter-master Corps!

Forsyth's second-in-command, still limping from a severe Civil War wound, was Lieutenant Frederick H Beecher, the nephew of Reverend Henry Ward Beecher. The scouts brought their own horses, but the Army provided them with guns and ammunition. About a third of the men were Civil War veterans. One of them, First Sergeant W H H McCall, by rights, should have outranked both Forsyth and Beecher. He had been a brigadier general of Volunteers.

The Fight Where Roman Nose was Killed

Early in September, Sheridan sent his new force into Colorado on patrol with a packtrain of four mules. Forsyth was on the heels of a large party of raiders, although he did not yet have enough men for the job. Those he did have, however, were tough and were very well armed with Colt revolvers and seven-shot Spencers. Few wore uniforms; most were in buckskins or other civilian dress.

On 16 September 1868 Forsyth's men pitched camp on the west bank of the 'Arickaree', the Arikara Fork of the Republican River. The stream had just gone dry after a summer of drout in the area of the Colorado-Kansas line. Just as Forsyth made his inspection next morning, a sentry shouted 'Indians!'

A war party of 600–700 Sioux, Cheyennes and a few Arapahos charged on carefully-selected war ponies. They

Above: The Hunkpapa chief, **Gall**.

medicine was good. Most of the whites' horses were killed. Wolf Belly made two passes along the fringe of willows without being hurt. Forsyth was down, hit in the right thigh, the left calf, and the scalp. As the first charge began to ebb, the wounded Major saw Beecher stagger and fall. As he died, the Indians regrouped and charged a second time and were again repulsed.

The Indians, now gun-shy, put off another charge even though they outnumbered the scouts about 14-to-one. They awaited the arrival of Roman Nose. The great Cheyenne warrior had violated a *taboo* by eating bread touched with metal (a fork) while visiting the Sioux. He had to make amends to the gods by purifying himself before his sacred and talismanic warbonnet would make him bullet-proof. He was a bit reluctant to join the fight, not sure that his 'medicine was good' again, meaning that he was not in the good graces of the great spirit. But, goaded by other Cheyennes, he painted his nose red, his chin black, his forehead yellow, and put on his magic 40-feather warbonnet.

Roman Nose led almost 500 pony soldiers in a third charge, planning to gallop right across the island, trampling the defenders into the sand. But the Spencers grew hot again and after the third and fourth volleys, ragged holes began to appear in the line of horsemen. Roman Nose was almost on the island, at the willow fringe, when a rifle ball smashed into his spine just above the hips. Someone later said that it was part of the sixth volley. The slug knocked him, mortally wounded, from his horse. He hid in the bushes until dark, then crawled to a bench of the stream that night and was carried to the top of a low hill on the right bank. There, where a historical marker is located today, he died in the night.

Forsyth took advantage of a breathing spell at nightfall to count his casualties. Of his original 51 men, seven lay dead, including Surgeon John H Mooers, or were dying. Seventeen more groaned with less serious wounds.

Next day, the Indians declined to attack. Roman Nose's death had taken away their desire to do battle. They settled down to starve Forsyth out. When he called for volunteers to go for help, every last ambulatory man came forward. He chose an ex-trapper, Trudeau, and 19-year-old Jack Stilwell to slip away in the darkness and get help from Fort Wallace, some hundred miles away.

On the third day, the Indians threw only a few rounds at the trapped men, letting the broiling sun do their work for them. The brave Forsyth, burning with fever, tended to his wounds. Carefully, he operated on himself—without any pain-killer—with his razor.

On the fourth day, the day that all rations gave out, the scouts saw the squaws break camp and leave. But the siege continued. By the fifth day of their entrapment, the survivors were so ravenously hungry that they cut hunks of flesh from the stinking, bloated, carcasses of their animals. One shot a coyote, another foraged some wild plums. The men dug deeper in the sandbar and brought up muddy water. In an agonizing decision, Forsyth decided to send out two more messengers, though it weakened his defense. The first pair, he guessed, were lying dead on the plains somewhere.

Now, the Major felt his own strength ebbing. He ordered all able-bodied men to leave the island and fight their way to safety if they could. Sergeant McCall led a 'mutiny', speaking for all of the scouts in rejecting the order. 'We've

were led by Tall Bull of the Cheyennes and Pawnee Killer, the Sioux. They were outraged that the whites dared to invade their hunting grounds although they had themselves sworn not to cross the Arkansas into the area.

Forsyth ordered his men to dig slit trenches with their knives and tin cups in the sand and gravel of a small island in the middle of the stream bed. The isle measured barely 20 by 60 yards, but its tall grass and willows offered some cover. Once they ran off two of Forsyth's pack animals, which carried valuable medical supplies and even more precious ammunition, the Indians maintained a galling fire from both banks and from downstream.

Suddenly the main body of Indians dropped down the banks and charged up the stream bed like a troop of cavalry. They hoped to kill all of Forsyth's horses, then run over the island and kill the plainsmen at leisure. Tall Bull ordered his horsemen to charge through the low morning mist together, like white men (as Roman Nose had taught him), and not fight lone actions to count coups—and lose a battle.

As if in imitation of the Wagon Box fight, Forsyth had his men hold their rifle fire to the very last moment. When the Indians were almost upon the island, the company gave them a fusillade that stunned them. The quick-firing Spencer rifles at only 50 yards cut the Indian force in two. But the Indians then surrounded the island and poured a heavy fire into it. For the moment, at least, Cheyenne

fought together and, by God, if need be, we'll die together.'

But Trudeau and Stilwell did reach Fort Wallace safely, the young soldier helping the exhausted mountain man, but Trudeau died at the fort. A messenger was sent galloping after Captain Louis H Carpenter, already in the field with a unit of the 10th Cavalry. Forsyth's second pair of couriers also arrived safely.

Carpenter pushed his black troopers hard, covering 100 miles to the river in just two days. On 25 September the eighth day of siege, the Indians pulled out for their sanctuary south of the Arkansas, unwilling to give the black 'Buffalo Soldiers' a fight.

When Carpenter dismounted on the bloody island, he found his old comrade, Forsyth, calmly reading *Oliver Twist*, though with his Spencer across his knees, ready for action. Later, the Major confessed to his friend that his supposedly gallant gesture was really a cover-up, to keep himself from breaking down in desperation in front of his handful of totally exhausted men who, almost out of ammunition, looked to him for leadership.

Forsyth was dizzy with fever. As if his three gunshot wounds were not enough, he had given himself blood poisoning with his crude surgery on himself with an un-sterile razor. It took Forsyth two full years for his body to recover from the beating that it took on **Beecher's Island**.

The Indians called the battle the Fight Where Roman Nose Was Killed. Some of the surviving scouts thought that they had killed 'hundreds' of hostiles. Perhaps they wounded 100. The toll admitted to by the Indians, six dead, seems much too low and Forsyth's not all that high, at 35 dead warriors.

Sheridan now, unfairly, canceled Forsyth's plan. He returned to the use of regulars, especially cavalry patrols from permanent bases.

In 1868, four years after being treacherously attacked at Sand Creek, Black Kettle presided over a flourishing village of 51 friendly-Cheyenne lodges on the Washita River 40 miles east of Oklahoma's Antelope Hills. Unsure of the protection of the Medicine Lodge Treaty, he asked General William B Hazen at Fort Cobb, 100 miles away, for permission to move his people closer to the protection of the post. The General told him not to worry. His village would never be attacked by whites.

Was Hazen lying? Like Sheridan, he saw Black Kettle's refuge as a 'cancer'. Both generals knew that the chief proclaimed peace but, at the same time, welcomed young braves back from raids into Kansas. They brought scalps, white captives, even souvenirs in the form of dispatches captured from Army couriers. Custer, of course, followed his mentor, Sheridan. His orders were to destroy villages and ponies, kill or hang all warriors and take women and children prisoners.

Right: **Philip Sheridan** was General William T Sherman's lieutenant in the West and his disciple. He believed in total warfare and had no sympathy for the Indians he fought. After service in Texas, California and the Northwest, he won great fame in the Civil War as a daring cavalry commander. Sheridan was sent in 1867 to the Department of the Missouri and there began the Army's practice of winter campaigns against hostiles. Colonel George Custer's strike at Black Kettle, the Battle of the Washita of November 1868, was one result of this new kind of Plains warfare. Sheridan's grand design was to drive cavalry units deep into Kiowa, Comanche and Cheyenne country when the Indians least expected it. His drastic measures worked, gaining peace at least temporarily. Sheridan fought in summer, too, and the Battle of Summit springs (11 July 1869) was the culmination of his 1868-69 campaign. He sent Major E A Carr and five companies of 5th Cavalry from Fort McPherson, Nebraska, after Tall Bull and his elite (Cheyenne) Dog Soldiers. Carr was supported by the 150 Pawnee Scouts of Major Frank and Captain Luther North. William F (Buffalo Bill) Cody was Carr's scout. Carr killed 50 of the enemy, including Tall Bull, and captured 117 at a cost of only one soldier wounded. Sheridan dumped the idea of using civilian scouts in force after Forsyth's siege at Beecher's Island (1868), but gave Colonel Ranald Mackenzie his head so that he chased the Kiowas and Comanches out of their Palo Duro Canyon hideout. Sheridan then sent Mackenzie crashing across the heretofore sacrosanct Mexican border in search of hostiles. In 1869 'Little Phil' was promoted to lieutenant general and given the Department of the Missouri. He, among others, was credited with coining the phrase 'The only good Indian is a dead Indian.' In 1870 he went to Europe as a military observer in the Franco-Prussian War. On Sherman's death in 1883 he took command of the Army. Sheridan always protected Custer and had him reinstated after his court-martial and suspension following the Hancock Campaign of 1867.

The Rising Star of George Armstrong Custer

Custer, the Boy General of Civil War days, was the natural choice to test Sheridan's new strategy of winter warfare, with poor Black Kettle his hapless first target. He would see to it that all Indians were given no rest during the worst season of the year when they were cold and hungry and their ponies worn out.

Sheridan fielded three columns to converge on the Canadian and Washita River valleys of Indian Territory. The main one was under his favorite. Custer led his 7th Cavalry out of Camp Supply, Indian Territory, after a last-minute conference with Sheridan. It was a below-zero morning but his spit-and-polish regimental band played the jolly air, 'The Girl I Left Behind Me'. Custer was young, handsome, dashing and brave. He was also politically as

well as militarily ambitious, a sometimes-dangerous combination. And, like his brother Tom, with whom he shared many a similarity, he was rash to a fault, reckless. But Sheridan liked this side of Custer. He thought that boldness was a good trait in a cavalry officer. However, even Sheridan feared that Custer lacked common sense.

George Custer was determined to make a comeback after an interruption of his brilliant cavalry career. He had been court martialed and suspended from duty for a year for cruelty to his men in the Hancock Campaign of 1867. At that time, he drove his men hard on forced marches without even stopping for water. Desertions became frequent and when 15 men lit out at a noon break, Custer ordered them brought back—but not alive. Five were recaptured, and alive. Custer's subordinates had refused to obey what they saw as a clearly improper order—to

Above: Some cavalry officers never forgave the callous Custer for failing to search for **Major Joel Elliott's** missing 16-man command at the Washita in 1868. The detachment was intercepted by Indians and destroyed to a man, the brave Sergeant-Major Kennedy being the last one to fall in the bloody snow.

murder. (One deserter-prisoner died of wounds, however.) The next day Custer hurried his regiment to Fort Wallace, then took 100 men to Fort Hays for supplies. He marched them 150 miles in 60 hours, giving them only six hours rest. Two stragglers were picked off by Indians. Finding no supplies, he pushed on to Fort Harker. Then, to compound his folly, he boarded a train to visit his wife!

Punishment was swift. In just ten days Custer was under arrest for leaving his regiment without orders, abandoning stragglers, shooting deserters and marching his men beyond endurance. The conceited and unrepentent colonel

Above: In spite of the fact that he was Custer's favorite scout, **California Joe** remains a mysterious figure. He was probably not from California and his name was not Joe, though he was identified by some as Joe Milner (or Milmer) and Joseph Hawkins. California Joe's name was Moses Milner. He became Custer's chief of scouts in the Washita campaign of Sheridan's winter war. Joe headed a detachment of scouts and delegation of friendly Osages when Custer left Camp Supply to attack Black Kettle. When Custer sent word of victory to Sheridan, he chose Joe to carry the message. With another scout, Milner got through enemy country at night and in record time. Astride his conspicuous mule, he then led his scouts in the grand review of Custer's troops, just ahead of the dejected Cheyenne prisoners and the regimental band playing 'Garry Owen.' He was still chief of scouts in the Black Hills Expedition of the summer of 1874. This reconnaissance of the sacred mountains of the Sioux led to the gold rush of 1876. Custer sent a dispatch – 'I have on my table 40 or 50 small particles of gold, in size averaging a small pin head, and most of it obtained from one pan.' Joe, still an Army scout, was killed on 29 October 1876, shot in the back by Tom Newcomb at Fort Robinson, Nebraska. Newcomb did not have to stand trial; there were no lawmen and no courts in the Sioux country at the time.

Below: The Amon Carter Museum's watercolor, *Indians Attacking,* by Charles M Russell is one of the most spirited paintings of Plains Indians combat by the artist in that Fort Worth institution.

Above: Custer hit a sleeping Cheyenne village on the **Washita River** of Oklahoma on 27 November 1868 in the major fight of Sheridan's winter war. Peaceful Black Kettle saw a repeat of Sand Creek, with the 7th Cavalry substituting for the Colorado Volunteers. As the battle wore on, Indian reinforcements joined the fray, forcing Custer to run and abandon Major Elliott's detachment.

said that his actions were necessary for the safety of the 7th. As for his conjugal visit, he told the court that General Sherman had given him permission to go anywhere he liked: 'To Denver, or to Hell, if I wanted to.'

Thanks to his loyal friend Sheridan, who needed him to fight Indians, Custer was reinstated before his sentence even expired. Transferred to command of the 7th Cavalry from duty at Fort Hays, he made it into a crack outfit. His troopers were mounted on matched horses. He had a special unit of sharpshooters. Proficient trumpeters and a regimental band boosted morale. The musicians often played 'Garry Owen', the traditional West Point song which Custer adopted for his regiment. Most of Custer's men revered him; some despised him. Almost no one was neutral or indifferent toward the vainglorious officer.

Battle of the Washita

For an elite outfit, the 7th Cavalry made a faltering start on Sheridan's winter war. Custer's Indian scouts got lost in a snowstorm. But the blond, long-haired colonel soon straightened them out with compass bearings. And his organizational gifts were apparent. Like Napoleon, he realized that an Army traveled on its stomach. Every night the supply train caught up with the column to give his men hot meals.

Above: **George Custer** was controversial as a Civil War 'Boy General' and remained so to his dying day. Talented but reckless and self-centered, he was finally the victim, at Little Bighorn, of his overconfidence.

After a punishing three-day march over snow covered, frozen country, Custer slowed his advance and sent his second-in-command ahead on a scout, or reconnaissance. Major Joel H Elliott's squadron found tracks of a large number of Indians—automatically a war party in Custer's eyes. Guided by an Osage scout, Custer caught up with Elliott and reconnoitred Black Kettle's camp, near today's Cheyenne, Oklahoma.

Black Kettle, on his arrival home, had called a council to give his people Hazen's assurances that they would never be attacked. The chief awoke just before dawn the next morning, 27 November 1868, to hear a woman crying, 'Soldiers! Soldiers!' Sand Creek must have flashed through the chief's mind as he grabbed his rifle and fired a warning shot.

Black Kettle waited at the ford, hoping to stop the soldiers and talk peace. But they enveloped the village from four directions. So, under the fluttering Stars and Stripes and white flag of peace, Black Kettle got on his horse and took his wife (wounded at Sand Creek) up behind him. They were among the first to fall in a hail of bullets.

Black Kettle's 14-year-old son died in hand-to-hand combat with Captain Frederick W Benteen. Warriors who escaped from their tents made for the brush and ravines to fight back. But it took Custer barely ten minutes to secure the village.

Holding Black Kettle's village now proved to be a different matter from capturing it. Indians flocked from a chain of neighboring camps in the Washita Valley. They soon outnumbered the regiment. Because it resembled Sand Creek, the **Battle of the Washita** has been called a massacre. But it was not a clear victory for Custer. He suffered few casualties, but his ammunition supply was insufficient for him to hold the site. In fact, he may have been saved from defeat by the opportune distraction of the Indians by the arrival of his seven supply wagons and mounted escort.

Custer reassembled the regiment to pull out. Elliott and his men were missing. The Colonel decided that he dared not look for them. (He would never be forgiven for this by some officers and men.) After burning the lodges as quickly as possible, with their 4000 arrows, 500 pounds of lead and an equal amount of powder, he shot to death most of the 875 captured ponies to hinder pursuit. He released his 53 women and children captives and left. It was becoming a difficult and dangerous situation.

Custer was erratic, perhaps half-fool and half-genius. With the valley crawling with hostiles, now thousands of them, he skillfully extricated his force from the jaws of a trap. He did not run like the wind, as the Indians expected. Instead, he reformed his outnumbered column and marched it boldly up the Washita, guidons flying proudly in the wind and the band booming out 'Ain't I Glad To Get Out Of The Wilderness'. The astounded Indians gradually withdrew before him as he feinted an attack on the next village. The Indians pulled still further back under the cover of closing night, letting the puzzling Yellow Hair past.

When Custer briefly halted at the next camp, the Indians recovered their poise and set an ambush for him. But he smelled it out and fooled them again, making a right wheel in the direction of his planned withdrawal route and eluding the ambuscade.

The Washita campaign 'made' Custer, despite comparisons with Sand Creek. His unorthodox bluffing tactics worked beautifully. He lost only Major Elliott, Captain Louis M Hamilton (Alexander Hamilton's grandson) and 19 enlisted men killed, and three officers and 11 men wounded. He is said to have counted 103 dead Cheyennes on the field. (But there were whispers that only a dozen or so were really warriors.)

Later, a patrol found the mutilated remains of Elliott and his men. Arapahos coming to help the Cheyennes had intercepted the platoon of 20 men and killed everyone.

To welcome Custer back to Camp Supply, Sheridan turned out the entire garrison in a formal review. The men of the 7th waved scalps, including that of the pathetic Black Kettle. Sheridan congratulated him for his efficient and gallant service in wiping out 'savage bands of cruel marauders'. He termed Black Kettle's camp 'the winter seat of the hostiles.'

Sheridan shrugged off his critics, assuming them to be, largely, churchmen—'good and pious ecclesiastics'—who, in their misguided compassion, abetted the merciless red murderers of innocent men, women and children.

Sherman, of course, supported Sheridan and Custer. He paid no attention to Indian Agent Edward W Wynkoop, who resigned his post in protest of Sheridan's policies, crying out that Black Kettle had been betrayed by the whites whom he had trusted. The arguments of such so-called Indian lovers were weakened by the relics of Cheyenne raids found in the *tipis* of the 'friendlies', along with four white captives, two of whom were put to death by the Indians during the melee.

Sheridan promised to feed Cheyennes who surrendered unconditionally, and most survivors of the Washita gave themselves up at Fort Cobb. He sternly warned them, 'You cannot make peace now and commence killing whites again in the spring.'

Above : There was often an element of social outing to Custer's campaigns, with ladies, relatives and civilians all mixed up with regimental officers, as when Custer took his ease under an awning at Fort Abraham Lincoln.

When the first Comanches surrendered to him, Sheridan coined a phrase that has rivaled Sherman's 'War is hell'. When he asked a warrior for his name, the man answered, 'Tosawi, good Indian'. Sheridan shook his head and replied, 'The only good Indian I ever saw was dead'. This was shortly polished into 'The only good Indian is a dead Indian', the Plains Army's philosophy.

Custer erected Fort Sill as a watchdog over Comanches and Kiowas while the Cheyennes concentrated around Camp Supply. He planned more winter operations but was immobilized by insufficient supplies and much more than 'adequate' rain and mud. The bad winter also forced Major Eugene A Carr to take his column back to Fort Lyon, Colorado. But the Government deemed Sheridan's winter campaign a success, unlike Hancock's preliminary round, largely because of Custer's Washita victory and a Christmas present-surprise. On the holiday, Major Andrew W

Evans beat the Comanches and Kiowas at Soldier Spring on the Red River's North Fork before winter forced him back to his base, Fort Bascom in New Mexico. The Indians, punished more by winter than by soldiers, now surrendered in droves at Fort Sill, where they were made to swear to keep the peace.

On 15 March 1869, Custer found two hold-out villages of Cheyennes on Sweetwater Creek below the Staked Plains. He seized four chiefs as hostages to trade for two white women captives and, by threatening to hang the four, persuaded all of the Indians to surrender.

Tall Bull still would not give up. He decided to join the Northern Cheyennes but struck at the Smoky Hill Trail on his way north. Major Frank North's Pawnee scouts found him and his followers on 11 July 1869 at Summit Springs. With North was a young scout, William (Buffalo Bill) Cody. The Pawnees alerted Major Eugene A Carr, who attacked Tall Bull's village from both east and west. He easily routed the villagers, most of whom escaped. But Tall Bull and 20 men fought on bravely from the cover of a ravine. The chief cut hand and foot holds in the wall of the ravine to climb up to a better firing position. He got off one

shot, ducked down, popped up his head to take aim again— and a rifle slug slammed its way into his skull.

Carr's victory ran the Dog Soldiers out of Kansas, at last, and cleared the Smoky Hill, Platte and Arkansas Roads, and the Union Pacific and Kansas Pacific rights-of-way of all hostiles.

Firmness had worked, but President-Elect U S Grant, the old soldier, did not listen to his friends, Sherman and Sheridan, but, surprisingly, to the proponents of a Quaker Peace Policy in 1869. He wanted Indians christianized, fed, clothed and taught agriculture on reservations so that they should become self-supporting farmers.

Red River War

Most Westerners, especially Texans, scorned Grant's peace program. They saw Fort Sill and other posts and Indian agencies as just places of refuge for the 'bloody Quaker pets' who raided the Lone Star State and adjacent territories.

But the Comanches always insisted that the Army started the Red River War on the South Plains. As one

Above: No one left a greater impression on the post-Civil War Army in the West than **General William Tecumseh Sherman.** He graduated from West Point in 1840 but, after seeing little action in the Mexican War, resigned his commission in 1853 to become a California banker. He was in command of the California militia in 1856 but resigned when the Governor failed to back him up in the Vigilantes crisis. His march through Georgia, to Atlanta and the sea, in the Civil War and his 'War is hell' quote, won him immortality. From 1866 to 1869 he was commander of the Dept of the Missouri, covering the entire Plains. He skilfully used the Army, much reduced after the Civil War, to protect lines of travel and communication. He believed in total Indian warfare, even more than his loyal protégé, Sheridan, and was an outspoken opponent of the Bureau of Indian Affairs and his old friend President Grant's experiment with a 'Quaker' peace policy toward the redmen. He believed that Indians guilty of atrocities should be severely punished and all others placed on reservations. He wanted Indian affairs transferred to the War Department. In May of 1871, on an inspection of the Texas frontier, Sherman nearly lost his scalp to a raiding party of Kiowas led by Satanta. They passed up his ambulance to hit the wagon train behind him and kill six teamsters. The close call convinced the General that severe measures were not just desirable but absolutely necessary. He had no trouble getting Sheridan to loose Mackenzie and Nelson Miles, of course, in the Red River War of 1874-75. They broke the strength of the Kiowas and Comanches. (Mackenzie swept them from their Palo Duro Canyon hideout, killed 1,000 of their ponies and kept the rest.) However, Secretaries of War Rawlins and Belknap limited Sherman's authority though he was General of the Army, 1869-84. He felt humiliated and powerless, but he removed his headquarters (1874-76) from Washington to St Louis to get out from under their thumbs. Sherman retired in 1883, having dominated the Army's policies and strategy in the West for almost 20 years.

Above: Custer discovered the fate of **Lieutenant L S Kidder's men,** finding their bodies in July 1867 on Beaver Creek, Kansas.

chief said, 'It was you who sent out the first soldier, and we who sent out the second.'

The Comanches' allies, the Kiowas, were just as reluctant to trade a free life on the wide-open plains, chasing buffalo, for a confined existence on a reservation, perhaps herding sheep. Like the Comanches, they hid behind the proviso of the Medicine Lodge 'paper' which guaranteed them the right to continue hunting bison between the Arkansas and Red Rivers.

After Custer's victory on the Washita, Sheridan ordered all Kiowas, Comanches, Cheyennes and Arapahos to surrender at Fort Cobb. All but the Kiowas obeyed.

Sheridan sent Custer to round up the delinquents.

Sheridan and Custer found Satanta's winter camp on Rainy Creek. Custer refused to take the hand offered in friendship. He was aware that Satanta was the murderer-kidnapper of the Box family in Texas in 1866, and that this was only one of several such crimes of which he was guilty. He curtly told all chiefs that they were under arrest. All but Satanta and Lone Wolf, though under close guard, managed to slip away from night camps on the march to Fort Sill. Sheridan swore that he would hang the pair if their people did not surrender themselves. They came in, and the General released the chiefs from custody.

Fort Sill kept a watchful eye on 2000 Kiowas and 2500 Comanches on the adjacent but spread-out reservation. War hero Ben Grierson's garrison was composed mostly of blacks who turned out to be pretty good cavalrymen. The Indians called them Buffalo Soldiers because of their dark, curly hair. The Indian Agent was a kindly Quaker, Lawrie Tatum, 'Bald Head' to the Indians. He skillfully won the release of many captured Mexican boys from Kiowa slavery without paying ransom. He just cut off rations till his 'wards' came around.

Satanta swore for Sheridan's benefit that he would follow the white man's path, raise corn, and kill no more whites. Like all of his tribe, he really spurned agriculture even more than the Comanches did. He was content to trade buffalo robes and jerky to the Wichitas, who actually enjoyed growing maize, or Indian corn. What Satanta really wanted from Tatum were rifles and ammunition. He said that he wanted them only for hunting, but when

General Hancock gave him a major general's uniform in 1867, he proudly wore it while running off the herd of stock at Fort Dodge.

The split between Kicking Bird's more peaceful Kiowas and Satanta widened after a great sun dance of 1870 on the North Fork of Red River. Many young men then rode off to kill Texans, especially buffalo hunters. Satanta, who had complained about the white man's waste in cutting timber, was aghast at the destruction of the buffalo. The commercial hunters were systematically wiping out the southern herd. He said, 'When I see that, my heart feels like bursting.'

Even Kicking Bird was driven to lead 100 braves on a raid into Texas with Lone Wolf, White Horse and old Satank. After goading Fort Richardson by capturing a mail coach, he gave a rescue force an all-day fight before letting it go. He then returned to the safety of the Fort Sill agency. That winter, Satank, grieving for a son killed in Texas, brought his bones home to lie in state on a platform inside a special holy teepee. He placed offerings of food and water at the foot of the scaffold so that his 'sleeping' son would not get hungry or thirsty on his far travels.

Satanta wanted the Fort Sill officers to stop the Iron Horse from coming to ruin the buffalo hunts. Satank, old and wise, grunted that *talk* was foolish. Destroy the settlers, he advised. Big Tree wanted to burn the fort, then kill the soldiers as they should scurry out like ants from a mound. In any case, young 'buffalo hunters' evaded Grierson's guards at the main fords of the Red River and raided into Texas that spring and summer of 1871.

Satanta was told by a medicine man, Mamanti or The Owl, of a vision of his driving Texans into the ground. The shaman led him, along with Big Tree and Satank, on a raid penetrating all the way to the Butterfield Stage Road between Forts Richardson and Belknap in Texas.

Lying in wait by the roadside on Salt Creek Prairie just west of Fort Richardson on 18 May 1871, the Kiowas spotted a lone mule-drawn ambulance. Officers and, of course, wounded men traveled in these light Army wagons. It was escorted by only a handful of troopers. But Mamanti would not let his comrades attack it. The visionary predicted a richer haul if they would wait. He seemed to be a perfect prophet, for the single vehicle was shortly followed by a train of ten Army freight wagons. Satanta blew his bugle as dreams of rifles and ammunition danced before his eyes.

The teamsters knew that the wild tooting was the work of no Army bugler. They formed a quick defensive circle, but the Kiowas broke it and killed eight of the 12 defenders. The others escaped in the brush as the Indians excitedly plundered the wagons. To their disgust, there were no arms or munitions, only corn. So they took only the 41 mules when they started back to the asylum of their reservation. In the ambulance was General William Tecumseh Sherman, on a tour of inspection. Satanta could have easily brushed aside his small guard of honor.

The Demise of Satank

When the escaping teamsters reached Rock Creek, Sherman ordered units of Ranald Mackenzie's crack 4th Cavalry to the train's rescue, but they were much too late. Sherman was furious when Satanta bragged to Indian Agent Tatum that he—not the shaman—had personally led the raid. 'If any other Indian comes here and claims the honor of leading the party, he will be lying to you, for I did it myself'. He then insolently demanded ammunition and arms for future raids.

Tatum was now disillusioned and joined the General in a plot to snare Satanta. He did so because he refused to be a party to the Kiowas committing 'murder in the first degree' with impunity.

Rather than risk an open fight with Satanta, Sherman determined to use deceit. He invited him to a Fort Sill council. Satanta came alone, though Sherman ordered the other chiefs to come too. Satank then came in, but only by force. Big Tree, suspicious, tried to run. But he was herded to the pow-wow. Lone Wolf, true to his name, arrived alone and late.

Satanta saw no women and children when he entered the fort, but his suspicion was not aroused because there were hardly any soldiers about, either. He did not know that Sherman had hidden armed men in various buildings and 10th Cavalry troopers, saddled up, just inside closed stable doors.

Sherman and Colonel Benjamin H Grierson waited in chairs on the porch of the commanding officer's residence. Their visitors sat on the floor. Sherman was insensed when the braggart chief again boasted of killing the teamsters. The General told him that he and all others responsible for the atrocity would be arrested and taken to Texas for trial. Satanta's response was to extract a revolver that he had concealed under his blanket. He warned Sherman that he would rather be shot than imprisoned in Texas. At a signal, the shutters of Grierson's windows now flew back with a slam, to permit the black troopers inside, to cover the Indians with their carbines. At the same time, the mounted troops left the horse barns and formed a line in front of Gierson's whitewashed picket fence.

It was a standoff. Just then, Lone Wolf showed up. He carried two carbines and wore a pistol. He boldly gave one of the carbines to a chief and his pistol to another, saying in a loud stage voice, each time, 'Make it smoke if anything happens'. And when he sat down, he noisily cocked his own carbine.

Cooly, Sherman continued his pacing on the deck of the porch, arguing and reasoning. Stumbling Bear stealthily notched an arrow and began to bend his bow, with Sherman his target. But another Indian deliberately jostled him and the arrow sailed harmlessly into space. Grierson wrestled Lone Wolf for his carbine as the latter took aim at Sherman. They sprawled on the porch. One of Sherman's officers brought the line of cavalry carbines up, hammers back, but Satanta and Sherman both shouted 'No, no!', and the guns were lowered.

An outbluffed Satanta submitted to handcuffing, along with Lone Tree and Satank. They were taken from the Fort Sill guardhouse on 7 June 1871 and sent to Jacksboro, Texas for trial. Each of two wagons had three guards and a driver. Satanta and Lone Tree, resigned to their fate, were in one vehicle. Old Satank, in the other wagon, began to wail his death song. The chant should have alerted his guards, but didn't.

Opposite page: Haughty **Satanta (White Bear),** decked out in an officer's coat and wearing a peace medal, was one of the most warlike of Kiowa chiefs. But he ended his days strangely; as an old man, he broke one of the strongest of all Indian taboos, committing suicide in 1878.

As his wagon approached a tree by a stream, Satank called out to his comrades that he would not pass beyond it. Somehow, he slipped out of his manacles, pulled out a hidden penknife and stabbed one guard in the leg and pushed him off the wagon. He grabbed up a carbine but it jammed as he levered a shell into the chamber. While he was trying to clear the weapon, the lieutenant in charge of the guard detail shouted to his men to fire. Corporal John B Charlton, on the other wagon, shot Satank. But he did not fall and continued trying to fire his gun, so Charlton shot him a second time.

The lieutenant halted long enough for Satank to die, but neither buried him or hauled the corpse along. Instead, he callously had his men roll the body into a roadside ditch.

The murder trial began on 5 July 1871 in the Jacksboro courthouse before a jury of cattlemen. The jurors rendered a guilty verdict, to no one's surprise, and the judge sentenced the Kiowas to hang. But Governor Edmund J Davis, probably yielding to political pressure from the Indian Bureau, commuted the death sentences to life imprisonment in the State Penitentiary at Huntsville.

Sherman was, predictably, furious. He became even more angry later, in August 1873, when Lone Wolf persuaded the Governor to grant the pair their freedom in order to win the cooperation of the Kiowas in the Indian resettlement program. Even Indian Agent Tatum was so disgusted that he resigned.

Quanah Parker and the Comanches

Meanwhile, young Kiowas joined Quanah Parker's Kwahadi band of Comanches in the Palo Duro country of the Texas Panhandle. They struck in October 1871 and caught Rock Station asleep, rustling 10 horses in one night.

The raid embarrassed Fort Richardson's tireless commanding officer, 31-year-old Colonel Ranald Mackenzie. Before the Civil War (in which Mackenzie was wounded three times), U S Grant had called him the most promising officer in the Army. Mackenzie's 4th Regiment was all that Custer's 7th Cavalry tried to be. The 4th had almost no deserters. It was not because the privates loved 'the Old Man' so much, though they did respect him. No, it was because the harsh disciplinarian's orders, like Custer's before his court-martial, were to bring in deserters dead or alive.

Mackenzie, 'Three Fingers' to the Indians because of a Civil War wound, was a first-rate Indian fighter, like Crook or Miles, but with a more dashing style. He was barred from invading the sanctuary of the reservations, but he learned how to handle another Indian refuge, the bone-dry Llano Estacado or Staked Plain. He took a Texas column to Fort Bascom, New Mexico, and back, working his way from waterhole to waterhole, just like an Indian. He also exposed, finally, the chief source of Kiowa and Comanche arms and ammunition, the Hispanic New Mexico traders called *Comancheros*.

On 29 September 1872 Ranald Mackenzie had his first revenge for his loss of face at Rock Station. From Fort Richardson he struck 262 Comanche lodges near McClellan Creek, a tributary of the North Fork of the Red. He killed between 30 and 60 men and took 124 women and children prisoners, burned the *tipis* and made off with a thousand ponies.

Even Mackenzie still had much to learn, however, and

Above: **Colonel Ranald Mackenzie** was a dashing cavalry commander like Custer, but with more common sense. He smashed the Comanches in the Red River War of 1874-75 and hit at Kickapoo raiders, deep in Mexico, while under secret orders. Mackenzie went insane in 1883.

Opposite page: **Quanah Parker** was Chief of the proud Kwahadi band of Comanches, who stubbornly refused to sign any treaty or go on any reservation (till the defeats of Adobe Walls and Palo Duro Canyon in 1874). His mother was the Comanche captive, Cynthia Ann Parker.

the Comanches in a counterattack on his first night camp recovered most of their horses and some of the troopers' mounts. But the Colonel got his hostages to Fort Sill, where he used them as leverage to get Mow-way's band back on the reservation. However, many of the latter's men stayed out with the rising star of Comanche fortunes, the half-blood, Quanah Parker.

Young Kiowas and Comanches who raided into Texas made the mistake of killing two Texans on their way home. Soldiers in a running fight near Fort Clark in December of 1873 killed nine of the Indians. One was a son of Lone Wolf, another casualty his nephew. The Chief swore revenge and emphasized this oath by burning his lodge, killing some of his favorite ponies, and cropping his hair in grief. Once that the grass was up in the spring of 1874, he took a party deep into Texas to recover the bodies of his young relatives. He skillfully avoided pursuits from Forts McKavett, Concho and Clark, but a patrol finally forced him to rebury the remains before he got all the way back to his reservation.

That same spring of 1874, the Comanches invited their Kiowa friends to a sun dance. Cautious Kicking Bird did not attend, but Kiowas Satanta and Lone Wolf were there. At the ceremony, the Indians expressed their hatred of 'buffler' skinners of the Staked Plain. With the connivance of the Army, the buffalo hunters killed more than three and a half million bison between 1872 and 1874 alone, while the Indians' toll was perhaps 150,000 animals. Sheridan, asked by Texans how to stop such a wasteful slaughter of such a valuable Plains resource, answered that he did not want it stopped. He believed that the deliberate extinction of the species was the *only* final solution to the Indian problem,

Above: **Satank** did not wait seven years, like Satanta, to die after being arrested. Satank's 'suicide' was condoned by Indians. En route to prison in Texas, he sang his death song, stabbed a soldier with a pen knife that he had hidden, and got his gun. He was shot dead before he could escape.

Left: Charles Russell painted a fine watercolor, **Smoke Signal**, now in the Amon Carter Museum in Fort Worth. It represented a party of scouts on an out-cropping of rock, their war ponies out of sight on the back slope of a bluff, as they exchanged signals with Indians on a distant butte.

to bring peace to the West and to 'allow civilization to advance' among the Indians.

At the unusual sun dance, not a Comanche tradition, a young Kwahadi prophet, Isatai, seconded the motion of Quanah Parker that they and the Kiowas go to war to save their buffalo. He would help. Not only did he promise to vomit up, literally, whole wagonloads of ammunition, as needed, he guaranteed to stop the white men's bullets in mid-air with his medicine, or magic.

Down from reservations in the north came Cheyennes and Arapaho allies to swell Parker's force to 700 picked men. Just before sunrise of 27 June 1874, Quanah Parker closed a noose of warriors around the tiny buffalo hunters' settlement of Adobe Walls near the Canadian River in the top of the Texas Panhandle. They killed and scalped two men who tried to escape in a wagon, then charged the settlement.

A few ponies stepped in prairie dog holes and sent their riders sprawling, but most got so close that they could poke holes in the roof of one building to shoot at men inside. But the 28 buffalo hunters behind adobe walls or forted up in the buildings, would not be frightened and would not be decoyed. They refused to be intimidated by odds of more than 25-to-one and wasted no ammunition in panicky rapid firing. After all, they were all armed with heavy, long-barreled Sharps or Remington (rolling block) buffalo guns of powerful caliber and deadly accuracy.

They shot Quanah Parker's horse out from under him, then as he took cover in a wild plum thicket, another heavy slug creased his shoulder. Another Indian later remembered, 'One of our men was knocked off a horse by a spent bullet fired at a range of about a mile. It stunned him but did not kill him'. This was probably the miraculous long shot by Billy Dixon.

Adobe Walls was perhaps *the* classic defensive action of all the Indian Wars, even more so than Beecher's Island. The valiant buffalo men lost just three of their number, one of them lanced by Quanah Parker himself. They managed to kill at least 15 warriors and critically wounded many more.

Naturally the Indians were annoyed with the discredited Isatai. A Cheyenne lashed him with a quirt, but Quanah Parker stopped the whipping. Lone Wolf and Satanta took their Kiowas back for the tribe's sun dance, inviting the Comanches to join them. One of the Comanches admitted, 'The buffalo hunters were too much for us.'

The End of the Red River War

The bested Indians took out their anger by terrorizing routes of travel in Kansas, burning, raping and killing till even the Indian Bureau stopped apologizing for them and Sherman was able to give Sheridan carte blanche on 20 July 1874 to turn his troops loose in an all-out Red River War against 4000 Indians, perhaps 1200 of them warriors.

During that summer of drought and grasshoppers, probably half of Fort Sill's Comanches and Kiowas drifted away to join Quanah Parker's Kwahadi Comanches in the hidden chasm of Palo Duro Canyon, the Panhandle's equivalent of Cañón de Chelly. The deep gash in the plain was invisible till one was right on top of it. Called the Place of the Chinaberry Trees, it had been seen by few whites since Coronado's time. Late in that summer of 1874, the Comanches, Kiowas and Cheyennes made it into an inner sanctum where they laid in supplies for winter.

Sheridan revised his tactics, shifting from scattered small patrols to five powerful columns closing in on the Staked Plains. Among his field commanders were Colonels Nelson 'Bear Coat' Miles and John W 'Black Jack' Davidson. The latter was sometimes eccentric because of an old sunstroke attack. And, of course, Sheridan employed Mackenzie.

There were skirmishes, one involving Billy Dixon of Adobe Walls fame. Because it involved a siege in a mud hole, it was called the **Buffalo Wallow Fight**. The 110-degree heat of August turned to September rain and mud. Surprisingly, Satanta and Big Tree surrendered.

As Mackenzie closed the ring on the Indians, he was the victim of a night attack on 26 September 1874. He beat it off and, this time, kept the marauders from stampeding his horse herd. In the morning, he took up the pursuit and his Tonkawa scouts found the Palo Duro Canyon hideout. One of the first to see it was Satank's old nemesis, John B Charlton, now a sergeant. He fetched Mackenzie.

The Colonel brought his whole column to the lip of the long defile at daybreak of the 28th. He could find no trail down to Prairie Dog Town Fork in the bottom, so he simply plunged down the steep slope at the head of his men.

Mackenzie's men swept the canyon, hitting Lone Wolf's Kiowas first. They were dismayed to find interlopers in their haven and fled like antelopes. Troopers pursued them and the other Indians for five miles. They caught only a few and killed only three braves—but only because the battle was such a complete rout.

Stealing a page from Carson's Cañón de Chelly campaign, Mackenzie did a masterful job of scorching the earth. He burned all lodges and precious winter rations, then drove 1424 ponies into the head of Tule Canyon. He picked out the very best animals for his men, then slaugh-

tered the balance, more than 1000 horses. This action virtually dismounted both tribes. Destitute, many Kiowas and Comanches were back on the reservation by October. At Christmas, most of Mackenzie's troops were in warm, snug, quarters.

Lone Wolf and about 250 Kiowas did not stop running till 25 February 1875, then surrendered at Fort Sill. On 2 June 1875, even Quanah Parker, who had scorned all treaties, was disheartened. He had to give up, ending the Red River War.

Sheridan made sure that it stayed ended. He sent 74 Indian leaders to the stone dungeons of ancient Castillo de San Marcos, Fort Marion, in St Augustine, Florida. He forced Kicking Bird to select Kiowas for exile, among them Lone Wolf and the shaman, Mamanti. The latter put a curse on Kicking Bird, who died mysteriously after drinking a cup of coffee. In just three months, the medicine man was, himself, dead in Florida, supposedly having willed himself to death in remorse for having killed his chief.

Satanta had violated his parole in joining in the war. After he surrendered at the Cheyenne Agency, 24 October 1874, he was put in the guardhouse in irons, then returned to Huntsville. In 1878 he succumbed to despair and committed suicide by throwing himself out of an upper-story window of the prison hospital.

About the same time, a malaria-stricken Lone Wolf was allowed to return to the West from Florida. He died within a year, ending the reign of the Kiowa and Comanche horsemen as Lords of the Southern Plains.

Ranald Mackenzie Sweeps into Mexico

In the spring of 1873 the energetic Mackenzie was transferred to the Rio Grande to put an end to raids into Texas from Mexico. The marauders were a few Lipans, many Mescalero Apaches, and a large group of Kickapoos. The last were emigrés from Kansas.

Mackenzie asked Sheridan for permission to cross the line and invade the Mexican sanctuary. Sheridan ordered him to do so, secretly (no records were kept), and when Mackenzie asked for explicit instructions, the general pounded his fist on a table and erupted, 'Damn the orders! You must assume the risk. *We* will assume the final responsibility.'

The Americans crossed the Rio Grande into Coahuila and attacked a Kickapoo village near Remolino, 40 miles west of Piedras Negras. Mackenzie's men swept through the camp, dismounted and fought their way back in again on foot. They killed 19 and took 40 prisoners, but mostly women, children and old men, since many of the warriors were away at the time of the attack. The Colonel had one man killed and two wounded. Before a collision could occur with Mexican troops, Mackenzie bolted for the border.

Mexico protested, of course, but Mackenzie was quietly praised by his government for a job well done. The Kickapoo lesson was not lost on the marauders. They lost some of their faith in the middle of the Rio Bravo stream bed. For three years, West Texas enjoyed a respite from Coahuilan raiders. When the attacks started up again, veteran General E O C Ord used Lieutenant Colonel William R Shafter and Mackenzie to repeat the lesson. In 1880, however, Mexican protests, dwindling raids and the removal of Ord ended the strictly illegal policy.

The Apache Wars Flare Up Again

Early in 1871, civilians re-ignited the smouldering Apache War in Arizona. Indian attacks led the Tucson *Citizen* and its readers to suspect Chief Eskiminzin's small band of San Carlos or Western Apaches of being guilty, even though these Aravaipa Apaches were seemingly peaceful and sedentary people, camping on Aravaipa Creek and the San Pedro River. The Chief had established a rapprochement with an enlightened commandant of nearby Camp Grant, Lieutenant Royal E Whitman. A lowly lieutenant could not make treaties, but he let the Indians stay rather than going to the White Mountain reservation of the Coyotero Apaches.

Whitman wrote to General George Stoneman for instructions, but his letter was returned. It was not in the proper form; he had neglected to summarize its contents on the outside of the envelope. The disgusted subaltern let the Indians stay where they were.

The Aravaipas turned in their guns, even their bows and arrows, settled down to planting corn and cooking mescal. Whitman paid them to cut hay for the post so that they could buy supplies. Nearby ranchers began to hire some of the men as cowhands. In the middle of March about 100 Pinal Apaches joined the Aravaipa experiment.

An old Indian fighter, William Sanders Oury, teamed with prominent Tucsonians to form a Tucson Committee of Public Safety. These Vigilantes, six Anglos and 46 Mexicans, then recruited almost 100 Papago mercenaries. On 28 April they set out to teach Eskiminzin a lesson.

An Army unit in Tucson warned Whitman of the danger to his neighbors and he sent messengers to the Chief to bring everyone inside the fort. He was too late. He recalled, 'My messengers returned in about an hour with intelligence that they could find no living Indians.'

The posse descended on the sleeping village about 4:30 am, raking the wickiups with fire and shooting down their occupants as they fled. It took the Vigilantes only half an hour to 'clean up' the village. The Committee held 27 captives, all children, who were handed over to the Papagos to sell as servants (that is, slaves) in Mexico.

Whitman found the burning village littered with stripped and mutilated corpses, bristling with Papago arrows and often with the heads smashed. Reports disagreed on the number of bodies—86, 115, 125, 145 and 150. Almost all of the dead were women and children. Some of the women had been raped before being shot. Children, even infants, had been shockingly hacked with knives as well as shot. A horrified Fort Lowell surgeon corroborated Whitman's description of the sickening scene. The lieutenant buried the dead, hoping that the Aravaipas would not blame him.

The Camp Grant Massacre was termed 'pure murder' by President Grant, who threatened to place Arizona Territory under martial law. It even shocked some Westerners, used to such atrocities. But Tucson was not ashamed. Instead of punishing Oury and Elías, his right-hand man, the townspeople called for the removal of Whitman for giving asylum to the Indians. And they nearly got it. He survived three trumped-up court-martial proceedings which were ultimately dropped. But after serving for years without promotion, he resigned his commission.

Elías considered the massacre of the innocent women and children as swift punishment of red-handed butchers, 'a memorable and glorious morning'. So strong was the

Above: The San Carlos Reservation agent **John P Clum** posed in buckskins with the Apaches **Diablo** and **Eskiminzin** in 1875 at the Agency. Eskiminzin was the victim of Arizona vengeance in the Camp Grant Massacre of 1871 when Mexican, American and Papago vigilantes destroyed his village, killing most of his people and forcing the remainder into the cruel bonds of slavery.

outcry in the East, however, by a press and public still mindful of Sand Creek, that the Vigilantes were brought to trial in December 1871. The trial lasted five days but the verdict, for aquittal of course, was brought in by the jury in just 19 minutes. This was so although the Camp Grant guide, sutler, beef contractor and mail carrier all backed Whitman's protests that the defendants' claim—that a trail of Apache raiders led directly to Aravaipa Creek—was false.

Grant relieved Stoneman and replaced him with Lieutenant Colonel George Crook, jumping him over 40 angry full colonels. The President also sent out peacemakers Vincent Colyer and General O O Howard, the humanitarian soldier who had lost his right arm in the Civil War. They chose four Apache reservations in Arizona and one in New Mexico. The locals derided Colyer as 'Vincent the Good', but it was Howard who dumfounded Crook, when he said that God meant him (Howard) to be the Moses of the American Indians.

The unkempt Crook, dressed in mufti or an enlisted man's uniform, was such a tough man that his appointment as Stoneman's successor to command the Department was applauded by most Arizonans. But since the eccentric behind the muttonchop whiskers tried to be fair, in his way, some critics were shortly calling him an Indian lover. Certainly his first words did not endear him to Arizonans, 'I think the Apache is painted in darker colors than he deserves.'

Crook added, however, that the Apaches had but two simple choices. They could settle down and cultivate the

soil, like Pimas and Papagos, or they could continue stealing and raiding—and be killed. The General saw his government's vacillating policy, misinterpreted as fear by the Apaches, to be fueling the fires of war. To put a stop to the tribe's traditional depredating, Crook meant to go after the Apaches in a 'sharp, active campaign' as soon as he could, to save millions of dollars and many, many lives, both white and red.

Crook was the perfect choice to bring the Apaches to heel. Of all the Army commanders, he was most like his foes. He thought like an Indian. In serving his apprenticeship in California, Oregon, Washington and Idaho, he had learned to fight Indians. He could also live off the land as they did. Like them, he knew the weaknesses of the army and frontiersmen—their politicking, drunkenness, revenge.

Soon, many Apaches turned themselves in. By the fall of 1873, 6000 were at least on reservation rolls. But Crook had to send cavalry into the Chiricahua Mountains to flush out one of their chiefs, Cochise. The Chief's old friend, Indian agent Tom Jeffords, got the Apache and Howard together and they came to an agreement. Cochise got the reservation that he wanted and the agent that he wanted—Jeffords. Cochise kept his word and kept the peace, but he fell ill and died in 1874, as Jeffords hurried to Fort Bowie for an Army surgeon to treat the chief.

Above: In the 1870s **desert Apaches** posed for a photographer. The U.S. government wanted to turn these fierce fighters into farmers. *Below:* **Mojave braves** photographed by O'Sullivan in western Arizona in 1871.

Above: **General George Crook** was the Army's worst-dressed officer, but its best Indian-fighter, even if the Sioux beat him on the Rosebud. Crook was very effective against the Apaches, fighting them as nearly as possible on their own guerrilla terms.

Crook hired Apache scouts in 1872 to track their hostile brothers that winter. He accepted no excuses for losing a trail. He replaced wagons with pack trains, and horses with mules trained to carry overloads—320 pounds, up from 175. And they had to march an extra 20 miles a day for him. The General wanted to be as mobile as his enemies. Unlike most officers, he was just as happy with infantry as horse soldiers, since the Apaches most often moved and fought on foot in their mountain territory.

On 15 November 1872 Crook invaded the Tonto Basin under the Mogollon Rim, hoping to catch his prey immobilized in winter camps. His orders were to find a trail and follow it to its end. If horses or mules played out, his men were to follow a foe on foot. Nine units scoured the basin and killed perhaps 200 Apaches in 20 separate actions.

Crook's ceaseless campaigning soon began to sap the Apaches' will. They were unable to sleep, to rest, to cook their mescal—for the smoke would surely bring Grey Wolf, as they called Crook. They could not hunt, except with bow and arrow, since gunshots brought troopers and Apache scouts even through the snow.

After Christmas, Crook's Apaches found a stronghold of Yavapais in a canyon of the Mazatzal Mountains, perhaps the band which, long before, kidnapped Olive Oatman in a classic Southwestern captivity. The scouts led Captain William H Brown's squadron of the 5th Cavalry, dismounted, through a cold night to a mesa commanding the canyon. A Lieutenant Ross and a dozen sharp-shooters went ahead with the Apache scouts, posting themselves in the canyon to support a dawn attack.

But the wan light of daybreak showed Brown that he had miscalculated. The enemy was not camped on the valley floor, but in a cave on a slope and on a rock shelf outside the opening. And the campsite was protected by huge boulders.

There was no time to change plans. Ross's marksmen opened fire, killing a half-dozen warriors with their first rounds. The major advanced 40 men to the lieutenant's position, then followed to bottle the Yavapais (called

Apaches by the soldiers) in what would later be dubbed Skull Cave.

The Indians refused to heed Brown's call to surrender or his offer of safe conduct of women and children. Again he had his men fire at the angled roof of the cave where it was exposed so that the rifle balls would ricochet into the cavern's defenders. The soldiers heard cries of pain. Again Brown asked for a surrender, but he received no reply, only a strange chant. His Apache scouts told him that it was the Indians' death song. He prepared for a charge.

As the Indians swarmed from the cave the soldiers opened fire from the shelter of the boulders. A few warriors retreated into the cavern, but most hid behind rocks on the ledge. Now Captain James Burns joined the fray from the canyon's rim, his men taking pot shots at the Yavapais below, even rolling boulders down on top of them like the Navajos fighting Pfeiffer in Cañón del Muerto.

After the great rocks tumbled in clouds of dust, Brown signaled Burns to stop. He then sent skirmishers scrambling up the slope. They hardly had to fire a shot. The silence was eerie. They found 75 'Apaches' dead or dying. Another 18, bruised and dizzied by the artificial avalanche, were taken prisoner.

Crook continued to send his officers on such expeditions even when epizootic fever took a heavy toll of his horses and mules. His foot soldiers simply carried everything on their aching backs.

At Turret Peak, south of Camp Verde, Captain George M Randall and a battalion of the 23d Regiment cornered Apaches on 27 March 1873 much as Brown had brought the Yavapais to bay. He had no artillery to blast them loose, so he sent his footsoldiers scurrying up cliffs—at midnight —to charge the enemy at dawn. Surprise was complete and the only escape for the Apaches was either surrender or hurling themselves to their deaths. Most preferred to become prisoners. Turret Peak broke the back of Apache and Yavapai resistance.

By the spring of 1875, Arizona Territory was peaceful. Crook was the hero of the hour. He took advantage of the hiatus in the fighting to improve roads and forts and to stretch 700 miles of telegraph wire over the Territory. Promoted to brigadier general, he was sent to command the Department of the Platte in 1875, to keep the Sioux from rebelling.

Red Cloud, after winning his personal war with the United States, had, surprisingly, accepted agency life and was, by 1873, the leader of the reservation Sioux on the upper White River of Nebraska. But he and Spotted Tail had trouble restraining their rambunctious young men, even with the presence of nearby Forts Robinson and Sheridan.

A much greater source of worry for the Army than malcontents on the Red Cloud and Spotted Tail Agencies was the roaming about of Crazy Horse, hero of the victory over Fetterman, and 40-year-old Sitting Bull. The ex-warrior still limped from a Crow bullet in one foot, but he was now an Indian politician, even a statesman. His influence extended beyond the ranks of his Hunkpapas and the Oglalas to all of the Teton Sioux and even to Cheyennes and Arapahos. He called reservation Indians fools for making slaves of themselves in exchange for fat bacon, hardtack and sugared coffee. Thanks to the likes of Sitting Bull and Crazy Horse, the Sioux were bound to explode into war again; the only question was when and where.

THE SIOUX CAMPAIGN AND THE BATTLE OF LITTLE BIGHORN

In the 1870s, the fierceness and tenacity of the Sioux had to be reckoned with, as the Army attempted to force them onto reservations. The climactic chapter in the conflict between the white man and the Indian began with General Sheridan's campaign in the summer of 1876, which led up to the Battle of the Little Bighorn. George Custer's disastrous defeat there was the most spectacular victory achieved by the Indians in the wars on the Plains and it was also the last major victory.

Above: **Black Hills** (Deadwood, SD) miners angered the Sioux in 1876.
Opposite page: The **Heroic Death of Custer**, showing Custer surrounded by downed men and horses on the hill above the Little Big Horn River, based on conjecture since there were no survivors from Custer's force.

Conflict intensified in the 1870s when the Army shifted its attention to the Sioux, the one tribe—aside from the Apaches—which seemed to pose a continuing, perhaps permanent, threat to Western settlement.

In 40-year old Sitting Bull, the Sioux now had a master politician as well as a war chief. In 25-year old Crazy Horse they found a natural military genius. And since he was married to a Cheyenne, ties between Sioux and Cheyennes grew stronger as war approached.

In 1873 Sitting Bull blocked surveys of a Yellowstone River route for the Northern Pacific Railroad. Twice, Lieutenant Colonel George Custer had to fight off Sioux assailants in tenacious encounters.

The next year, 1874, Custer explored the Black Hills, a sacred area to the Sioux. The hills had been ceded to them in 1868 as their land 'forever,' part of the Great Sioux Reservation. But some of Custer's men found gold in the Black Hills and miners began to prospect its streams by the summer of 1875. The Army removed the pioneer party of miners from Gordon's Stockade, near modern Custer, but others only followed. So many men slipped past patrols that a gold rush occurred as public pressure to open the hills to legal white settlement increased. The Army was soon swept aside and, to the anger of the Sioux, Custer City and Deadwood became boomtowns reminiscent of California's Mother Lode of 1849.

That same year, George Custer's brash young brother, Tom, captured a rising Hunkpapa, Rain In The Face. The warrior later made his escape, swearing that he would eat Tom Custer's heart.

The Government offered to pay the Sioux six million dollars for their holy mountains. Some Indian leaders were amenable to selling the Black Hills, in any case lost to them already, but they wanted five times that paltry sum. Others would not hear of selling the sacred place for any price. So, between the railroad building and the Black Hills gold rush, the Sioux drifted back onto the warpath, ignoring the Government's orders to return to the reservation.

BRITISH
COLUMBIA

NORTHWEST TERRITORIES

ONTARIO

WASHINGTON
TERRITORY

Bear Paw Mtn
(1877)

■ Ft Benton

MONTANA

Ft Union

DAKOTA

MINNESOTA

Portland

Ft Walla Walla ■

Willow Springs (1878)

● Helena

Ft Missoula ■

TERRITORY

Ft Keogh

Ft Abraham Lincoln

OREGON
TERRITORY

Whitebird
Creek
(1877)

● Butte

Big Hole (1877)

Canyon Creek (1877)

Ft Custer

Little Bighorn (1876)

Rosebud (1876)

Sioux Wars
(1854-90)

WISCONSIN

Minneapolis ● St Paul

IDAHO
TERRITORY

Ft Bridger ●

Ft Phil Kearney ●

TERRITORY

Ft Pierre

● Deadwood

● New Ulm

Lava Beds (1873)

Modoc Wars
(1872-73)

Dull Knife (1876)

Ft Fetterman ■

Wounded Knee (1890)

Chicago
(Missouri Military
Division HQ)

Sacramento

WYOMING
TERRITORY

Ft Laramie ■

NEBRASKA
TERRITORY

Omaha ●

IOWA

San Francisco
(Pacific Military
Division HQ)

● Reno

NEVADA
TERRITORY

Salt Lake City ●

Cheyenne ●

Thornburg Massacre (1879)

Meeker Massacre (1879)

● Ft Kearny

ILLINOIS

UTAH
TERRITORY

Leadville ●

● Denver

Cripple Creek ●

Ft Leavenworth ■
Ft Riley ■

KANSAS

Independence ●

● St. Louis

CALIFORNIA

COLORADO
TERRITORY

MISSOURI

Ft Defiance ■

Ft Supply ■

INDIAN

ARIZONA

● Taos

■ Ft Union

Santa Fe ●

■ OKLA

Apache Wars
(1881-1900) ■ Ft Apache

● Okmulgee

TERRITORY

ARKANSAS

■ Ft Yuma

Tucson ●

Geronimo Surrenders
(1886)

NEW MEXICO
TERRITORY

El Paso ●

STAKED PLAINS

■ Ft Sill

Ft Worth ● Dallas
●

MEXICO

TEXAS

LOUISIANA

San Antonio ●

Major Battles in The West
(1876-1890)

● Cities
■ Forts
✕ Battles
Military Division of the Pacific
Military Division of the Missouri

Above: **Sitting Bull (Tatonka-I-Yatanka)**, the Hunkpapa Sioux leader, was photographed in feathered headdress by David Barry in 1885.

Above: A freckled Colonel (and Brevet General) **George Armstrong Custer** posed for the great Civil War photographer, Mathew Brady.

By the time that the proud Centennial Year of 1876 rolled around, to be celebrated with a great world's fair in Philadelphia, the Sioux and Cheyennes were preparing a celebration of their own. It would show their independence of the Great White Father in the East and his Long Knives on the Western Frontier. By 1876, 50,000 Indians were in rebellion. Only 15,000 were bona fide warriors, and probably no more than 4000 took the field against the bluecoats.

The 1867 Campaign on the North Plains — Retreat at Powder River

The War Department sent its very best man, Crook, to put down the Sioux and their Northern Cheyenne allies. He had ten companies of cavalry and two of infantry. His field commanders were polar opposites—the reckless Custer and the timid Alfred H Terry. Crook was supposedly only an observer in the field, but usurped command from his nominal expedition head, Colonel Joseph J Reynolds. He did not want to be slowed down, so he left his 80-odd wagons behind (also his pack-mule train) as he hurried out of Fort Fetterman on a clear 1 March.

On the **Bozeman Trail** the Bighorn Expedition found a more formidable foe than even the Sioux. A series of northers roared down the trail, freezing the troopers although they were bundled up in long underwear, blanket-lined overcoats, fur caps and buffalo robes.

Reynolds, on the point of Crook's column, halted his advance when his scouts reported a Cheyenne and Sioux encampment in a cottonwood grove under the bluffs of Powder River. He tried to surprise the Indians, but a young herder gave the alarm. The Colonel's squadrons drove into the village only to meet a punishing rifle fire which turned them back. Reynolds dismounted his men in the village and had them dig in as the advantage shifted to the attacked. The Colonel had the Indians' food supplies and pony herd, but warriors on the bluffs pinned down the soldiers with a steady fire.

Reynolds lost his nerve and ordered a retreat back to the main force. He let the Indians retake their ponies and he moved his men out so fast that he left behind either two dead men or one dead trooper and one wounded man—the latter to be tortured to death by the Sioux. (His total losses were two dead and six wounded.)

Crook was furious with Reynolds. He abandoned the advance in order to return to base and prefer charges against him.

Crook's Sioux campaign of 1876 had begun poorly. His Crow scouts reported that the humiliation of Reynolds on Powder River had greatly increased the recruiting of warriors by Crazy Horse. Unknown to the Army, it would face in the Rosebud-Bighorn country the greatest concentration of warriors in the entire history of America's Indian wars.

The Battle of the Rosebud

After refitting, Crook left Fort Fetterman again at the end of May with more than 1000 cavalrymen and infantrymen and almost 50 officers. He had many teamsters and

Above: The artist titled this picture **Desperate Charge of General Crook's Cavalry at Battle of Rosebud.** Crook had little chance to charge the enemy there, because he was preoccupied with organizing a retreat to avoid being overwhelmed by the Indians. He was hours on the defensive when the Sioux, tired or bored – but certainly not beaten – pulled out. Crook tried to call it a victory, but retreated and stayed put for eight weeks, bandaging wounded and begging for reinforcements. The Sioux, free of restraint, helped crush Custer at the Little Bighorn.

packers, too, and he carefully armed them as auxiliaries. In the field, he added Crow and Shoshone scouts, 262 of them. His column was one of three comprising Sheridan's pincers movement in imitation of the successful Red River campaign of 1874 and 1875.

The General wanted to split the rumored large force of Indians into several smaller bands, then deal with them separately. So he had Colonel John Gibbon move eastward from Montana to make contact with General Alfred Terry (and Colonel Custer), moving westward from Fort Abraham Lincoln. As the columns converged, Crook, moving northward, would roll back the Sioux on the Terry–Custer column.

Crook leapfrogged his strung-out column along the dusty Bozeman Trail, sending his infantry ahead, but soon to be passed by the horse soldiers. Both reached bivouacs ahead of the supply train and rearguard. When he entered hostile territory in mid-June, Crook halted his wagon train under a strong guard of 100 infantrymen, then made 200 of their companions into mounted infantry or quasi-cavalry, to take along. At Tongue River a courier from Sitting Bull and Crazy Horse warned him not to cross a symbolic line scratched in the dirt. If he did cross, he would have to fight. This suited Crook perfectly.

believed the casualty count of Chief Scout Frank Grouard, instead—28 killed and 56 wounded. The neutralizing of Crook by Crazy Horse, who lost no less then 36 dead and 63 wounded in the fray, guaranteed Custer's utter defeat at Little Bighorn. Gibbon and Terry would eventually meet, but it would be too late to save the 7th Cavalry.

The Battle of the Little Bighorn

The heart of Terry's force was Custer's 7th Regiment. Some of the Colonel's officers were real fighters—Captains Frederick Benteen, Myles Keough and Tom Custer. (George's brother, Tom, had won not one but two Medals of Honor in the Civil War.) But Colonel Custer's second-in-command, Major Marcus A Reno, though a Civil War veteran, was untried in Indian warfare. While Gibbon camped on the Yellowstone at the mouth of the Rosebud, Reno scouted the Powder and Tongue River valleys. Terry's base was the mouth of Powder River.

Terry called a pow-wow in the cabin of the steamer *Far West* on 21 June to outline his strategy to Gibbon and Custer. He was worried that he could not catch the enemy in order to defeat him. He wanted Custer to time his cavalry attack so that Gibbon's slow-moving infantrymen would be in position in the north to block any flight of the Sioux. Terry issued written orders so that there would be no misunderstanding his plan. This was to bottle up the hostiles in the Little Bighorn Valley between Custer and Gibbon.

Custer, in buckskins, led between 600 and 700 horse soldiers. His Arikara scouts did not know the country, so he borrowed six of Gibbon's Crows. But he declined Terry's offer of four troops of the Second Cavalry and a Gatling gun platoon. He did not want to be slowed down by the horse-drawn artillery and he certainly did not want his beloved 7th Cavalry to share victory honors with the Second Regiment.

The stage was set for the debacle when Crazy Horse engaged Crook at Powder River, forcing him to pull back. And the ambitious Custer was much more overconfident than the plodding realist of Apache campaigns.

Custer was later accused of direct disobedience of orders. There is no doubt that he bent them badly, ignoring Terry's instructions to ascend the Rosebud to its head before turning west after the Indians, whose trail had been found by Reno's scout. (This delay would give Gibbon's foot soldiers time to get into position to support the cavalry in the Little Bighorn Valley.) Instead, when the hostiles' trail left the Rosebud for the Little Bighorn drainage, he followed it. This rashness compounded his initial mistake of underestimating terribly the number of his foes. A tragedy of errors was thus set in motion.

To be fair to Custer, not even his Indian scouts dreamed that he was opposed by such enormous numbers of warriors. He had chosen the single moment in history when 3000 braves, at the very least, were gathered to fight together. Many were armed with Winchester repeating rifles against the troopers' single-shot Springfield carbines. And, for once, the Indians' strategy was to stand, and not fall back into one of their usual running fights. Finally, the warriors were led by such men as Sitting Bull, Crazy Horse, Gall and Rain In The Face.

Custer knew that the Indians had spotted him and were, probably, aware of his strength. For his part, he was com-

General Crook knew the Apaches much better than he did the Sioux. He was surprised—his troops enjoying a coffee break—on the morning of 17 June on the Rosebud. Only the splendid fighting of his Shoshones and Crows prevented a disaster. Never was conflict fiercer than in the broken terrain, terrible for cavalry or even any kind of concerted battle plan. Several troops were roughly mauled and gave way. Crook sent Anson Mills to seize Crazy Horse's village (which he mistakenly thought lay just to the north). With his main force so battered, Crook wisely called off Captain Mills. The latter swung around behind the hostiles and forced them to abandon the battlefield. This led Crook to claim a victory in the Battle of the Rosebud, since he was left in possession of the battle site.

Actually, Crook was humbled by Crazy Horse. Though he admitted to only ten dead and 21 wounded, many

Above: **Custer's Last Stand**. A lithograph by Otto Becker made in 1895. The red-haired Custer (center) slashes dramatically with his sabre. In fact Custer had been armed with two revolvers and was sabreless. Incredibly, the soldiers were mostly armed with single-shot rifles, not repeaters such as the Spencer or the Winchester, which greatly reduced their volume of fire.

pletely unaware of the fact that he was outnumbered five to one. He had not even been able to see the Indian village from a high point he called **Crow's Nest**. (Actually, the Indians occupied a series of populous villages in the valley of the Greasy Grass.) But, once more, ego and ambition overruled prudence, even common sense.

If Custer ever considered a withdrawal, which is unlikely, it was probably too late to effect it now, in any case. So he decided to smash straight through the enemy, but this time, incredibly, he guaranteed disaster for himself by fragmenting his regiment. Leaving one troop (company) to guard the pack train, he kept only five for himself. Suicidally, he split off three troops under Benteen in a scout to the south and three more with Reno. The latter was to chase a party of 40 Sioux into the upper end of the village. He promised to support the Major with 'the whole outfit.'

Custer, however, hesitated after his promise to Reno, then apparently changed his mind. Rather than riding to his support, he veered off to the north to strike the lower end of the village.

Everything went wrong. Reno charged as ordered, but could not make a dent in Chief Gall's huge force. There was no sign of Benteen, supposedly ahead of him, or of Custer supporting him from the rear.

Reno did the best that he could with just 112 men. He retrieved his men from the outskirts of the village, where Sioux swarmed like angered ants from a nest. He dismounted his troops in a patch of timber, but Indians infiltrated his line. Seeing a trap closing on him, he ordered his men to remount and fell back across the stream to dig in on a bluff above the river.

Reno's withdrawal, sane enough, was held against him in the later court-martial in which he was used as a scapegoat for Custer's disaster. He had lost only a couple of men, so far, and may have panicked. Some say that he led the retreat instead of covering it from the rear. Worse, some of his troopers were left behind, trapped in the cottonwoods. A lieutenant wanted to go back for them, but Reno forbade it, as Indians counted coup by dragging soldiers from their mounts as they splashed through the shallow Little Bighorn. Quickly the toll began to rise. In just 45 minutes on 25 June 1876, Reno lost half of his command in dead, wounded and missing.

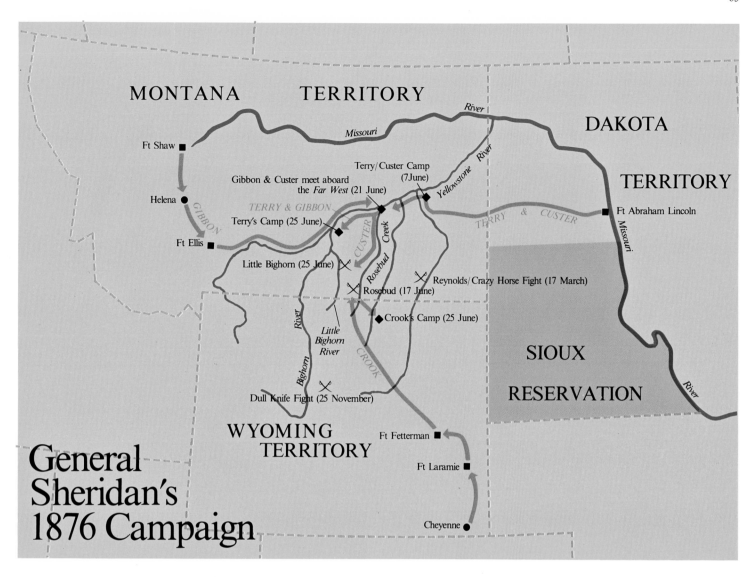

MONTANA   TERRITORY

Missouri   River

DAKOTA

Ft Shaw

Terry/Custer Camp
(7 June)

Gibbon & Custer meet aboard
the *Far West* (21 June)

TERRITORY

Helena

TERRY & GIBBON

Yellowstone River

Ft Abraham Lincoln

Terry's Camp (25 June)

TERRY & CUSTER

Ft Ellis

Little Bighorn (25 June)

Reynolds/Crazy Horse Fight (17 March)

Rosebud (17 June)

Missouri

*Little
Bighorn
River*

Crook's Camp (25 June)

SIOUX

RESERVATION

Dull Knife Fight (25 November)

General
Sheridan's
1876 Campaign

WYOMING
TERRITORY

Ft Fetterman

Ft Laramie

Cheyenne

River

Meanwhile, Custer came in sight of the first village and found it to be an armed camp. He rushed a courier to Benteen, ordering him to join him and to bring extra ammunition. 'Bring packs! Bring packs!' he scribbled on the note that he gave to his orderly. Custer then charged, but soon hauled up in the face of overwhelming odds and led a withdrawal to a high grassy ridge. It was Gall who pushed him back, but now Crazy Horse struck from the north while another force left Reno's shattered command to be in on the kill.

Benteen topped a rise and saw soldiers surrounded on a bluff. He took them to be Custer's men, so he galloped to their aid. So it was that the captain kept Reno from being overrun. When both officers heard shooting from downstream, they knew that Custer was also engaged.

Reno did not know what to do. Should he risk going to Custer's aid, as some of his officers insisted, now that he was reinforced? Or should he stay put in his defenses? After all, Custer was supposed to come to the support of his second-in-command, not vice versa. But Custer had ordered Benteen to reinforce *him*, not Reno. And the latter, at least on paper, had a stronger force, six companies, than his commanding officer.

Finally, a captain who was either very brave or foolhardy, Thomas B Weir, could no longer tolerate Reno's inaction. Against the latter's orders, he began to ease his way back down the bluff to the Little Bighorn. Benteen followed Weir's troop and, grudgingly, Reno gave the command to follow suit. But progress was very slow, since

Indian rifle fire continued. Also, the wounded had to be carried in blankets for want of stretchers.

Helping Custer was a forlorn hope at best. Reno's force was too battered. It was too late, anyway. Crazy Horse, apparently employing more Cheyennes than his own Sioux, had already surrounded and destroyed Custer's entire command. It took him only an hour. Crazy Horse was helped by Gall after he split his force, but easily kept Reno and Benteen pinned down while assaulting Custer at the same time.

'Custer's Luck' was over, forever. Every man of his command was killed and most were mutilated by the victors. Rain in the Face, as he had promised, cut out Tom Custer's heart and ate of it.

Crazy Horse and Gall turned to destroy Reno and Benteen. They easily chased them back to their bluff. The troopers fought well to save their lives but, even in rifle pits, they suffered 18 more deaths and had 43 wounded. Enemy fire did not slacken until nightfall, when the besieged soldiers watched a wild scalp dance below them, illuminated by the glare of campfires. In the darkness the officer and 16 men trapped in the copse of cottonwoods slipped safely through Reno's lines.

With the first light of dawn, the siege was tightened. Benteen and Reno had to throw back two assaults. Bravely, Benteen led a few counterattacks to keep the Sioux and Cheyennes at a respectable distance.

That evening the Indians withdrew, setting a grass fire to screen their movements. Their scouts had spied the

approaching relief column of Terry and Gibbon. The puzzle is why they did not swamp Reno and Benteen, or harass Terry. For the only time in history, they had sufficient warriors to do the trick.

Terry had been alerted by his scouts to the disaster. Ironically, Reno and Benteen as yet did not realize that Custer's force had been destroyed to the last man of the original 215. The Army buried the dead, took 52 wounded men in wagons, and fell back to Fort Abraham Lincoln. Reno's casualties were 47 killed and 53 wounded. Estimates of Indian losses ran all the way from 30 to 300.

The shock waves of the Custer calamity rippled across the entire country from the grassy plains of Montana and Dakota to New York, New Orleans, San Francisco. The Army looked for a live scapegoat since the real blunderer, Custer, was now a dead hero and martyr. Reno seemed to be a good bet because of his vacillating. He was censured and a court of inquiry found that he had done less for the safety of his men than certain subordinates. This was true enough. But the decision of the court was that there was nothing in his conduct, otherwise, deserving reproach.

Above left; David F Barry photographed **Gall,** the Hunkpapa Sioux warrior, holding a bow and arrow at Fort Buford, ND, in 1881. *Above:* **Rain in the Face** (1835-1905), photographed by F Jay Haynes, was the Hunkpapa who bragged that he would kill Captain Tom Custer and eat his heart – and presumably did so at Little Bighorn.

Nevertheless, a humiliated Reno took to drinking, was court-martialed in 1880 and dishonorably discharged.

Grant blamed Custer for the needless sacrifice of so many men. Sherman agreed, stating that Custer should never have broken his regiment into three pieces in the face of overwhelming numbers of Indians—even in such unconventional warfare as that practiced on the Western plains. Sherman also correctly laid some of the blame on Crook's mismanaged pincers move and retreat a week before Custer's Last Stand.

The First Scalp for Custer

One of the many myths surrounding Custer's calamitous last campaign is that the Army was momentarily paralyzed by the destruction of its crack cavalry regiment and most broke so fast for the safety of the reservation that Yellow Hand was the only fatality. (There were a few Indians wounded.) So the skirmish has come to be called the 'First Scalp For Custer.'

Crook was more annoyed with Merritt for his tardiness than pleased at his success at **Warbonnet Creek**. With him, he now had 2000 men and when he joined Terry, their combined strength was almost 4000. Naturally, Sitting Bull and his followers were not about to tackle such a formidable force. The chiefs spurned another open fight and broke up their temporary army into the usual small bands.

Crook did not repeat Custer's mistake of breaking his force into parts. But Terry tired of the chase and shortly disbanded his expedition. Crook persevered, though his men, exhausted by cold and muddy going, were almost out of rations. His campaign was now being called the Horsemeat March.

Crook's loyal aide, Lieutenant John G Bourke, described the command as 'a brigade of drowned rats.' Lieutenant Colonel Eugene Carr called Crook and Terry 'two fools' who did not know their business. The Shoshones apparently agreed. Chief Washakie took them home. Cody left, too.

The Battle of Slim Buttes

The first real opportunity to revenge Custer, if Warbonnet Creek did not count, came by accident. Crook sent Captain Anson Mills and scout Frank Grouard, with four officers and 150 men on the soundest horses, to bring back 61 pack-mule loads of food from Deadwood. Near **Slim Buttes** in the northeast corner of South Dakota, they stumbled on a Sioux village of 37 lodges. Mills sent a messenger back to Crook and waited in a drenching rain until daylight.

The villagers were completely unprepared for Mills's attack. Most scattered madly to the hills, though a few, led by Chief American Horse, fled to a box canyon and dug in. American Horse shouted warnings that Crazy Horse would soon come to rescue him. Mills appropriated the Indian food in the village and penned up the hold-outs in the dead-end gully till Crook should come to his assistance.

Crook arrived before the regrouping Sioux could counterattack against the game Mills. He posted vedettes on the hills to keep a sharp watch for Crazy Horse as rifle fire raked the ravine. Finally, American Horse gave up. He was shot, and was holding in his intestines with his hands. He died in the lodge that Mills turned into a makeshift hospital tent.

Even with Crook's mounted pickets, the Sioux suddenly exploded out of a pine woods as the soldiers relaxed over their first decent meal in days. But the Indians would fight only from a distance, and they withdrew after a day of long-range fire against the rear guard. Because of the aborting of Mills's supply mission, Crook was in no shape to pursue them. Again he sent Mills to Deadwood. This time the Captain returned with a herd of cattle and wagonloads of flour, bacon, coffee and hardtack, just as the column staggered up to the edge of the Black Hills.

Slim Buttes was hardly an answer to Little Bighorn. It was no smashing, decisive, victory. But it improved morale by ending the Army's string of reverses.

Guards at the reservations were reinforced and Colonel Ranald Mackenzie skillfully disarmed and dismounted the followers of Red Cloud, allowing Crook to replace him

Above: Custer and his Arikara scouts.

brilliant commander. True, Terry and Gibbon patiently waited for reinforcements. But Crook, also in the field, was joined by a new man, young Colonel Wesley Merritt, commanding the Fifth Regiment of Cavalry. Before meeting Crook, Merritt intercepted one of the many bands of Indians joining Crazy Horse because of his great triumph over Custer. It was 17 July, barely three weeks after the Battle of the Little Bighorn, when Merritt took on 800 Cheyennes who had just taken off from the reservation.

Merritt fooled the Cheyennes by setting up an ambush on Nebraska's Warbonnet Creek, sometimes mundanely called Hat Creek. He did so by posting snipers in the draws and cramming 200 hidden soldiers inside his apparently unescorted wagons. The Indians charged right into the young Colonel's trap. The skirmish, however, amounted to pretty much of a duel between Merritt's scout, Buffalo Bill Cody, and Chief Yellow Hand, sometimes identified (like Custer) as Yellow Hair. In a knife fight which has become legend, Cody killed his opponent. Lone Wolf's warriors

Above: At the Cheyenne River Agency in 1881, **Red Horse** drew a pictograph of Miniconjou Sioux warriors advancing against whites (out of sight) at the Battle of the Little Bighorn in 1876. *Below:* Horse skulls, ribs and other bones made the **Little Bighorn Battlefield** an ossuary. The photographer's view was westward down the slope of Custer's Hill to the river, the site of a Cheyenne camp on 25 June 1876 (see map right). *Below: right:* A detail of **Red Horse's** pictograph that recorded how warriors closed in on Custer's doomed command, with some of his men already decapitated or otherwise mutilated by the blood-lusting braves.

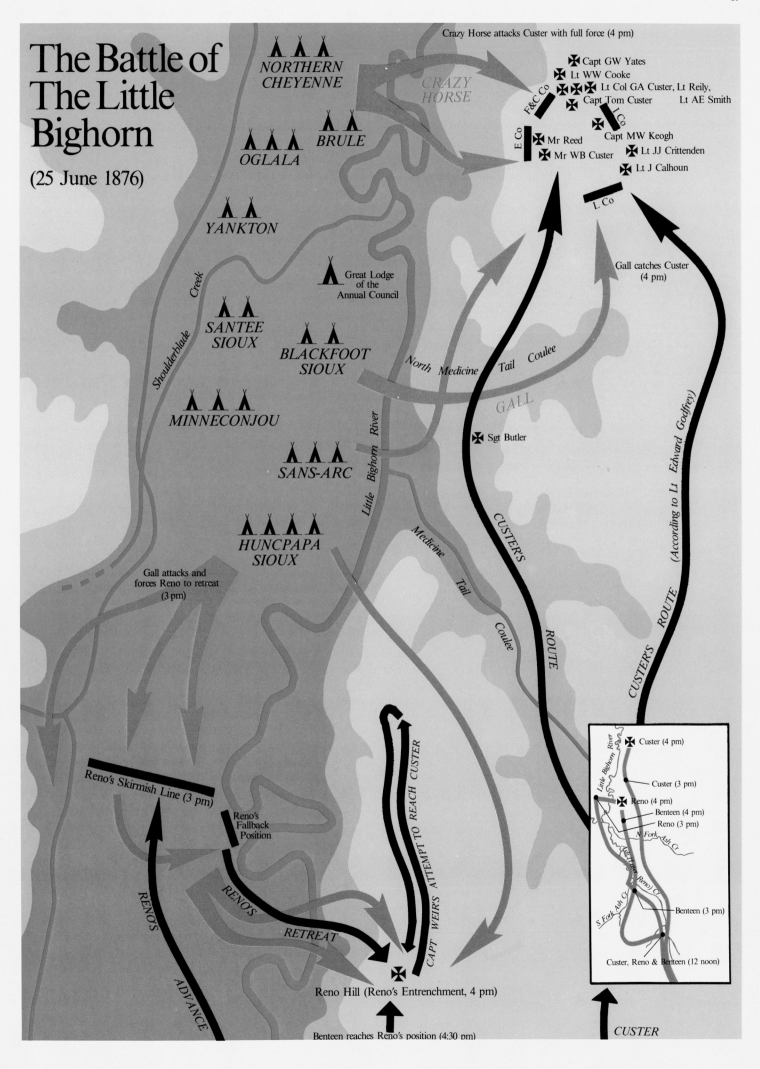

The Battle of The Little Bighorn

(25 June 1876)

NORTHERN CHEYENNE

BRULE

OGLALA

YANKTON

Great Lodge of the Annual Council

SANTEE SIOUX

BLACKFOOT SIOUX

MINNECONJOU

SANS-ARC

HUNCPAPA SIOUX

Shoulderblade Creek

North Medicine Tail Coulee

Little Bighorn River

Medicine Tail Coulee

Crazy Horse attacks Custer with full force (4 pm)

CRAZY HORSE

✠ Capt GW Yates
✠ Lt WW Cooke
✠ Lt Col GA Custer, Lt Reily,
✠ Capt Tom Custer   Lt AE Smith

F&C Co

I Co

E Co

✠ Mr Reed
✠ Mr WB Custer

✠ Capt MW Keogh

✠ Lt JJ Crittenden

✠ Lt J Calhoun

L Co

GALL

Gall catches Custer (4 pm)

✠ Sgt Butler

CUSTER'S ROUTE

(According to Lt Edward Godfrey)

Gall attacks and forces Reno to retreat (3 pm)

Reno's Skirmish Line (3 pm)

Reno's Fallback Position

RENO'S RETREAT

RENO'S ADVANCE

CAPT WEIR'S ATTEMPT TO REACH CUSTER

Reno Hill (Reno's Entrenchment, 4 pm)

Benteen reaches Reno's position (4:30 pm)

Little Bighorn River

✠ Custer (4 pm)

Custer (3 pm)

✠ Reno (4 pm)

Benteen (4 pm)
Reno (3 pm)

N Fork Ash Cr

S Fork Ash Cr

Benteen (3 pm)

Custer, Reno & Benteen (12 noon)

CUSTER

Above: Braves like **Short Bull** were proud of their fancy breastplates.

with the more peaceable Spotted Tail as chief of all of the Sioux. The Government then forced the tribe back to the Black Hills.

The Winter Campaign of '76

In October, Colonel Nelson Miles met with Sitting Bull. The talks broke down after Sitting Bull told the Colonel that God had made him an Indian, but not an *Agency* Indian. Miles then beat the Chief with his 'walk-a-heaps' (infantry) in a running battle that began in a grass-fire set by Sitting Bull. It progressed to a hasty hollow square defense, as the Sioux turned savagely on their pursuers, and extended over two days and 40-odd miles to the Yellowstone. Shortly, Miles took some chiefs hostage and forced 40 lodges to surrender, then chased Sitting Bull until December.

Crook, seemingly rendered almost as timid as Terry himself by Custer's debacle, put together a large army—too large for effective work—and marched up the Bozeman Trail into the teeth of a mid-November blizzard. He was after Crazy Horse, but when a scout reported a Cheyenne encampment, he sent Mackenzie for a look.

The doughty Scotsman led a thousand horse soldiers across the snow-covered Wyoming plains to arrive in position on a fork of Powder River on the bitter cold eve of Thanksgiving Day. The Cheyennes of Dull Knife and Little Wolf were having a celebration of their own, a victory dance after striking the Shoshones.

As usual, Mackenzie waited for dawn before attacking. He surprised his adversaries completely, driving all 400 warriors from the village. He killed off most of their ponies and fired the skin lodges after he found grim mementoes of

Custer's defeat in them. In stubborn—savage—fighting, the Indians battled back from river bottom, valley, slope and rim and almost won the day. But the superb fighting of Mackenzie's Indian scouts, and another of Crook's remarkable marches of reinforcements (26 miles in 12 hours) gave the victory to Mackenzie.

Some Cheyenne survivors were sheltered in Crazy Horse's Sioux camp, but most who did not freeze to death in the 30-below weather, without food, blankets, horses or shelter, chose to surrender. No one knows how many died of exposure, but Dull Knife lost 40 men in the battle itself, and had many others wounded. Mackenzie had one officer and five enlisted men killed and another 26 men wounded.

So severe was the weather at year's end that Crook had to call off the winter campaign of 1876 in late December. But 'Bear's Coat' Miles was not ready to quit. He almost got the surrender of Crazy Horse's huge village (600 lodges, 3500 people), over the Chief's objections on 16 December. But the Colonel's Crow scouts attacked the Sioux peace delegation. A furious Miles punished the Crows by dismounting them, and sent the Sioux the Crow ponies as an apology and payment for the five emissaries killed.

Proof that Miles's peace overture had misfired was a Sioux attempt to draw soldiers into ambushes. Miles was ready to play the game, even with his tired infantry. He followed the decoys after disguising two of his cannon as supply wagons. He was lucky. He captured some Cheyenne women and children, including a few relatives of Crazy Horse. That evening, 200 of the would-be ambushers tried to recapture the prisoners, but the colonel was ready for them. He prepared carefully for a battle on the next day and his hunch was right.

Shortly after daybreak of 7 January 1877, Crazy Horse himself led 500 Sioux and Cheyennes in an attack across country covered with several feet of snow. Miles heard Crazy Horse shouting in English, 'You have had your last breakfast!'

Because of the snowy and steep terrain, Miles could flush the Indians from positions atop steep bluffs only by a frontal assault. The overconfident Sioux and Cheyennes let the sweating, freezing, soldiers struggle up the slope in their burdensome buffalo coats. But before the Indians could wipe them out at close range, Miles unlimbered his disguised artillery. The Indians did not run, but were taken aback by this lively cannon fire. The leader of the assault, Major James S Casey, got a foothold atop the bluff. The battle seesawed back and forth till Chief Big Crow fell. The Indian defenses began to collapse.

A blizzard kept casualties low on both sides, but the Indian allies withdrew from the Battle of Wolf Mountain. Miles, short on supplies, turned back to the Tongue River Cantonment. From there he boasted to General Sherman, and to all who would listen, of his prowess. He compared his success with Crook's so-so showing. He suggested that Generals Pope and Terry be sent packing. He wanted an Army department all for himself; he was not content with his new District of the Yellowstone.

Miles bragged to Sherman that if given departmental command, and only half the troops there, he would end the Sioux War in four months, and 'once and forever.'

Sheridan and Sherman were annoyed by Mile's boasting. But they recognized his achievement by enlarging his District of the Yellowstone to include Crook's Powder River country, and by giving him more units to command.

As the new year opened, Sitting Bull said that he was calling off the war. He invited the Sioux to accompany him to the land of the Great Mother (Queen Victoria). Those Sioux and Cheyennes who did not follow him decided to scatter. Some went back to the reservations. Spotted Tail persuaded virtually all of his people to opt for peace, not war, by April of 1877. On 6 May, even Crazy Horse came in, throwing his three Winchesters on the ground, in sign of surrender, at the Red Cloud Agency. Most of the Indians surrendered to Crook, thanks to Spotted Tail. This angered the jealous Miles. But revenge would be his. He would go after the last hostile band, that of Lame Deer, the Chief who had vowed never to surrender.

Sioux and Cheyenne on the Move

Miles took as scouts such recently-surrendered Sioux and Cheyennes as Hump, White Bull and Brave Wolf. They found 50 lodges on Muddy Creek, a tributary of the Rosebud. A dawn charge on 7 May 1877 scattered the Miniconjous. Miles slaughtered half of their pony herd of 450 head, keeping the others to mount four companies of infantry. The Colonel counted 14 Sioux dead on the field. He lost four men killed and had one officer and six men wounded. But he nearly lost his own life in the battle's aftermath.

Hump, a Miniconjou Sioux himself, persuaded Chief Lame Deer and his head warrior, Iron Star, to surrender. They laid their rifles down and were grasping the hands of the colonel and his adjutant when a scout rode up and covered them with his rifle. Thinking that he intended to shoot them, the two 'renegades' grabbed up their own weapons. Lame Deer fired at Miles, at almost point-blank range. The Colonel dodged, in time, but the shot killed a cavalryman behind him. The warriors ran up a hill, but both were shot down.

Fugitives drifted in that summer and fall as Miles built two strong posts in the very heart of the Sioux nation to prevent any repetition of Little Bighorn. General Sherman visited Fort Carter (the other was Fort Keogh) and prophesied that the Dakotas would never regain their country. He was right, but he was premature in assuming that the Sioux War was over. The shrewd Sitting Bull had fled to Canada, but Crazy Horse was perceived as only biding his time before going on the warpath again.

Above: The camera caught **General 'Bear-coat' Miles**, fourth from left, sporting a fur cap, as he and scout **L S 'Yellowstone' Kelly**, mounted, prepared a winter pursuit of Crazy Horse in Montana. Dressed in cumbersome buffalo coats, the infantry faced extremely harsh weather conditions during this rugged campaign.

Crazy Horse was angered by rumors of a forced move of his people to a Missouri River reservation and offended by the Army's use of Sioux scouts against the Nez Percés. Crook, fearful that Crazy Horse's temper was nearing the flash point, ordered him arrested. He was taken into custody, but when both soldiers and Indians tried to disarm him, 7 September 1877, he fought them. Crazy Horse received a stab wound that proved mortal. To this day, it is not known for certain whether a soldier's bayonet or an Indian's scalping knife killed him.

Red Cloud and Spotted Tail, with Crook's support, talked President Hayes into granting them reservations west of the Missouri. Some of Crazy Horse's followers fled into Canadian exile with Sitting Bull. But most of the Sioux settled down in 1878 on the Rosebud and Pine Ridge Agencies. These were the old Spotted Tail and Red Cloud Agencies.

Homesick Northern Cheyennes on the Indian Territory reservation that they shared with the Arapahos bolted on 7 September 1878. Troops converged on Dull Knife and Little Wolf as they headed north. After hot-headed warriors killed civilians in direct disobedience of the chiefs' orders, Dull Knife and Little Wolf split. The former led his people to Camp Robinson to surrender; the latter kept on toward the Yellowstone.

In a sad affair foreshadowing Wounded Knee, the Army ordered the surrendered Cheyennes back to Indian Territory. When they refused, offering to go to Pine Ridge only, the commander of Camp Robinson tried to starve and freeze them into submission. He cut off all food, water and firewood. After a week of suffering, the Cheyennes made their break. With a handful of arms concealed by the women, they shot their barracks guards and fled into the January snow of 1878. The garrison soon overtook the weakened Indians and killed almost half of them—men, women and children. The Government, shamed by the stupidity and brutality of the enforcement of a bureaucratic decision, now yielded. Dull Knife was allowed to take his survivors to the Pine Ridge Agency.

Right: A detail of Frederick Remington's typically vigorous narrative painting, **Through the Smoke Sprang the Daring Soldier**, depicting cavalrymen in a snowy line of defense as a brave fellow goes 'over the top' in a one-man charge.

Little Wolf remained at large till 27 March 1879, when he surrendered. Miles signed his warriors on as Army scouts and after service at Fort Keogh, the Northern Cheyennes were allowed to drift back to the Tongue and Rosebud. In 1884 they were finally given a reservation of their own, the Lame Deer Agency near the Muddy Creek battleground.

Sitting Bull

Sitting Bull was still a source of serious worry to the Army. He and Gall and other chiefs built up a colony, just across the Canadian border, of 4000 Sioux and Nez Percés. The North-west Mounted Police kept an eye on them from Fort Walsh, but had no trouble, thanks to firm but fair dealings with the Indians. When the strain of feeding so many exiles taxed the Canadian buffalo herds, an attempt was made to return the Sioux to the US. But the Army's choice of General Terry as a commissioner doomed the initiative. The Sioux embraced the Mounties, but would not even shake the hand of their enemy. Sitting Bull accused Terry of coming only to tell lies and shouted, 'We don't want to hear them!'

Miles, scornful of Terry and as vain and ambitious as ever, was apparently ready to risk an international incident by invading Canada to grab Sitting Bull. Sheridan and Sherman tried to keep him away from the border, but failed when the Sioux, unwisely, moved across the line to hunt buffalo. Miles hurried to collar them on Milk River. An indecisive fight between his scouts and Sitting Bull's own hunting party was ended by Miles's arrival with new Hotchkiss rapid-fire cannon. The colonel pursued Sitting Bull and expelled a few hundred *métis* or 'Red River half-breeds' who supplied him with ammunition. But, to the immense relief of Sherman, he halted at the border, then pulled back to the Missouri to end his expedition. This act of sanity led Sheridan and Sherman to join Terry in showering praise on the bellicose Miles.

As the buffalo herds dwindled, hunger forced most of the Sioux to return to the US in 1879 and 1880. The last to surrender was, predictably, Sitting Bull. It was 19 July 1881. The Army would not let him live freely with his people, but kept him under house arrest at Fort Randall for two years. Sitting Bull's surrender symbolized the end of the Sioux Wars, except for the aberration of Wounded Knee, almost a decade later.

Miles was rewarded for his success by being given a brigadier general's rank and command of the Department of the Columbia at the end of 1880. A first-rate regimental commander and a dogged, able, field campaigner, he had easily out-performed Crook, of whom the Army expected so much. His use of infantrymen to wear down Sioux and Cheyennes led to a Congressional debate over the merits of cavalry versus footsoldiers. But, actually, the innovative Miles used a mix of cavalry and footsoldiers and often turned the latter, at least temporarily, into mounted infantry. Like Crook, he used Indian scouts skillfully, too. The Sioux had finally met their match not in the flamboyant Custer but in the indomitable Miles.

THE DEFEAT OF THE INDIANS AND THE END OF THE FRONTIER

The saddest and most unnecessary of all Indian wars, surpassing even the Modoc and Seminole affairs, was the Nez Percé War. It was absolutely uncalled for. For 70 years after the Nez Percés took the hand of Meriwether Lewis in friendship (1805), the tribe remained at peace. It was its proud boast that it had never drawn the blood of whites.

In 1863 Washington had planned to move two bands of these staunch friends from their ancestral homes on Idaho's Salmon River and Oregon's Wallowa Valley to a Lapwai Reservation in northwest Idaho. Old Chief Joseph fought back—without violence. His people came to be called 'non-treaty Nez Percés,' but he pointed out that Governor Isaac Stevens's 1855 treaty extended the reservation to include the Wallowa Mountains. He had refused to sign only the outrageous pact of 1863 which would have stripped away those lands on which gold had been found.

In a Presidential order, Grant in 1873 conceded that Chief Joseph (who died in 1871) had been correct. But the executive order was revoked only two years later because of the outcry of land-hungry Oregonians. The Wallowa Valley was designated a part of the public domain and thrown open to settlement. The younger Chief Joseph continued his father's work, but negotiations stalemated in late 1876.

The Nez Percé Campaign of 1877

One-armed General O O Howard was a humanitarian who sympathized with Joseph. But his hard-line Christianity led him to confuse Joseph's spirituality with a forerunner of the Ghost Dance, the Dreamer cult of Smohalla—who called for extermination of all whites. Reluctantly, Howard advised that force be used if persuasion should fail.

The Army tried to avoid being the scapegoat of the Indian Bureau, but was ordered to occupy the Wallowa Valley and did so. Chief Joseph gave in and began to move

his people to the reservation. But drunkenness had debauched some of his young men and they went on a whiskey-fueled spree in which about 20 settlers were killed. Joseph wanted to explain to Howard and to continue to the reservation, but his people persuaded him to join White Bird's people on the Salmon River.

Howard sent Captain David Perry, a Modoc War veteran, with three officers and 90 cavalrymen to prevent further attacks. He made a grueling night march in the mountains to cut off the Nez Percés before they could cross the Salmon River. Perry started his tired men down the steep canyon of White Bird Creek on 17 June 1877. At the mouth of the 3000-feet deep gorge lay Chief Joseph's lodges. The Chief meant to gather his stock there and, avoiding war, to move east to the buffalo plains as his people had done, seasonally, for centuries.

Joseph decided to talk peace with Perry, but to prepare for a fight, should it become necessary. He sent away his women and children, even his horse herd. Chief Joseph had only between 60 and 70 effectives. An equal number of warriors were sleeping off the huge drunk.

Captain Perry's men were preceded by a force of volunteers which opened fire on Joseph's truce party in spite of its white flag. The Nez Percés returned the fire with such deadly marksmanship that Perry's charge never got rolling. Instead, the volunteers fled and exposed his flank. Soon the Nez Percés were chasing the 1st Cavalry up the canyon. At the top of White Bird Hill, Perry attempted a stand, but had to fight his way back to the settlement of Mount Idaho on Camas Prairie. In killed alone, the Captain lost an officer and 33 soldiers. Joseph had no warriors dead and only three wounded.

General Howard now took personal command of the pursuit of Chief Joseph, but sent Captain Stephen Whipple to capture Chief Looking Glass, who was (so far) neutral. Whipple planned to parley but, like Perry, let his volunteers determine the action. They shot up the village, captured 600 ponies, scattered the unprepared Nez Percés—and drove Looking Glass into Chief Joseph's arms.

Chief Joseph skirmished with Whipple and volunteer

Opposite page: Handsome—if scarred—**Plenty Coups**, with earrings, shell bead necklaces and tomahawk typified the Army's Crow allies.

Above: Chief Joseph, in his masterful 1877 retreat toward Canada, and a possible link-up with Sitting Bull's exiled Sioux, had to penetrate the Blackfoot country of north-central Montana. Luckily, he did not run afoul of any war parties of **Piegans**.

units, then joined Looking Glass on the Clearwater. There Howard found them with their 800 followers, including 300 fighting men. It was 10 July 1877 and the Nez Percés were besieging a force of civilians. General Howard attacked, but soon found himself on the defensive as warriors swarmed up ravines and bluffs to force him back from the valley rim to an open prairie. **The Battle of the Clearwater** was a desperate one, but Joseph made the mistake of fighting it on the Army's terms instead of in his hit-and-run style. In a pitched battle of seven hours' duration. Nez Percé sharpshooters were no match for howitzer bursts and raking Gatling gun fire, even though the Indians captured Howard's pack train and, temporarily, some of his artillery.

Howard later said that the Nez Percés fought as well as any troops that he ever saw, but they were finally outflanked and driven from the field. They crossed the Clearwater and fled northward. Howard was too bloodied to pursue. He had 15 men dead and 25 wounded, to Joseph's four dead and six wounded.

The Battle of the Big Hole

While the Nez Percés took Looking Glass's advice and marched, via Lewis and Clark's old Lolo Trail, across the rugged Bitterroot Mountains, Howard built up the strength of his force for the pursuit. The Nez Percés planned to hunt buffalo on Montana's plains and perhaps join the Crows. If necessary, they were ready to trek to Canada to join Sitting Bull. Howard finally moved out after them on 30 July with 560 cavalry and infantry, 25 Bannock scouts, and 150 packers and other citizens with his 350-mule pack train. As Joseph struggled over the Lolo Trail, described by General Sherman as one of the worst routes for men or beasts on the entire continent, Howard telegraphed ahead for forces to intercept Chief Joseph in his flight.

A mixed bag of 150 regulars and quasi-militiamen fortified the pass by which Chief Joseph would exit from the mountains. His scouts sniffed out the whites, of course, and Joseph asked for permission to pass, promising that no harm would be done to settlers. When his request was refused, he tied up the strongpoint with desultory rifle fire and slipped his main force around it on secret Indian trails. Once he bypassed the defensive position, derisively called Fort Fizzle by Bitterroot Valley people who traded with the Nez Percés, he picked up speed in more open country.

But, still unaware of Howard's use of the 'talking wire,' Chief Joseph gave in to Looking Glass's demand that they rest in Montana's Big Hole Basin. Their people were tired and wanted to cut lodge poles. They had had no shelter since the Clearwater fight.

Colonel John Gibbon, the Sioux War veteran, heeded Howard's telegraphic appeals and brought 15 officers and 146 infantry in wagons, plus 45 volunteers, and caught the native military genius napping. Joseph felt so secure on 9 August on the Big Hole River, because of the lead that he had built up over Howard, that he neglected to post sentries.

The dawn attack took Chief Joseph completely by surprise. He lost his campsite in just 20 minutes. He and Looking Glass regrouped their marksmen in riverside thickets, however, and brought Gibbon's attack to a standstill. The Nez Percés outfought the whites in hand-to-hand

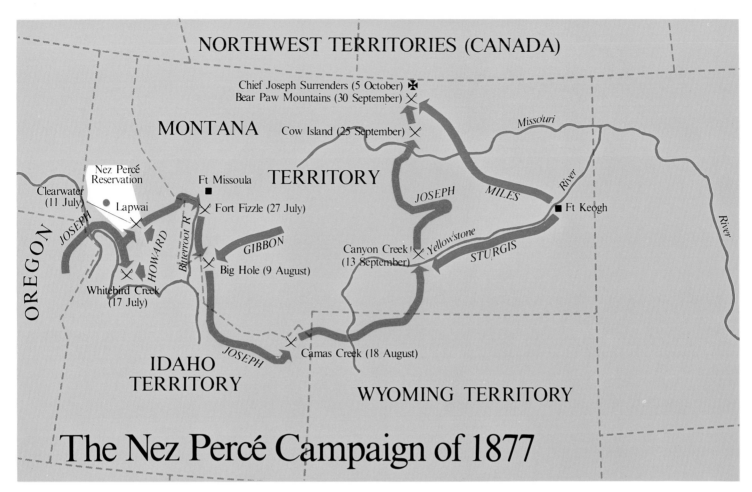

NORTHWEST TERRITORIES (CANADA)

The Nez Percé Campaign of 1877

assaults and the colonel wisely retreated from such a ferocious foe. The tide of battle changed so completely that soon Gibbon was pinned in a patch of timber, from which he sent a messenger to Howard for help.

Next morning, while troopers 'feasted' on raw horse meat in the woods, Joseph seized the Army's laggard supply caravan, disabled the Colonel's howitzer, and captured 200 very welcome rounds of ammunition. Sergeant Milton K Wilson bravely recovered the ration wagons, but the fighting dragged on all day, with Gibbon, himself, being wounded. Joseph exploited a wind to light a grass fire to cover his advance, but the wind shifted and burned itself out. Before the Chief could attack again, his scouts alerted him to Howard's approach and he pulled his men out of action.

Howard broke Joseph's siege of Gibbon, but it was an expensive victory for the Army, costing 32 dead and 37 wounded. But the **Battle of the Big Hole** was much costlier to Joseph. Gibbon had nothing to be ashamed of. Joseph lost 87 people, some of them women and children, but mostly warriors he could not spare.

Gibbon's force was too shattered to follow Chief Joseph as he re-crossed the Continental Divide into the Lemhi Valley of Idaho, where the formation of militia companies led the Nez Percés to kill some civilians. But Howard took up the chase immediately and soon was less than a day behind his quarry.

The End of the Trail

When Joseph turned on Howard on 19 August, he pulled off one of the most astonishing stratagems of the war. He personally led 45 of his 200 men straight—and noisily—at Howard's camp at Camas Meadows. He imitated a cavalry column of fours. Sure enough, the sentries mistook his party for Lieutenant George R Bacon's force, returning from Targhee Pass. They let the horsemen pass. When a guard finally gave the alarm, Joseph was driving off 150 of Howard's pack mules and some of his picketed cavalry horses.

Three troops galloped out at first light, just as Joseph hoped, and rode into his trap. He had regrouped his four columns into three, drawn up in an ambuscade. Two troops got out, but Howard had to rescue the third with a loss of one man killed and seven wounded.

Almost leisurely now, Chief Joseph withdrew through Targhee Pass, abandoned too soon by Howard, and into Yellowstone National Park on 22 August. That volcanic wonderland had already seized the public's imagination and, alas, the Nez Percés terrified tourists in the Park and killed two of them.

Howard, halted at Targhee Pass, was temporarily demoralized. He was unable to catch Joseph with his ragged and discouraged soldiers, many of whom were ill as well as exhausted. The general rode to Virginia City, Montana, for provisions, then telegraphed Sherman that he thought he ought to stay where he was. Sherman told him to pursue the Nez Percés to the death, 'lead where they may.' So Howard resumed his pursuit.

From the Little Bighorn country of bloody memory came Colonel Samuel D Sturgis with six troops of Custer's rebuilt 7th Cavalry. He was followed by Colonel Wesley Merritt with units of the Fifth Regiment. Joseph simply feinted toward the Stinking Water, or Shoshone River, to draw Sturgis there, then nipped along Clark's Fork to reach the open plains, making the Colonel look like a fool.

A mistake of Joseph's scouts now hurt him. Receiving incorrect reports that his direct route was blocked, the

Above: In 1877 F Jay Haynes made an excellent photographic portrait of *Chief Joseph* (1832-1904) of the Nez Percés, probably the most distinguished and humane of all Western warriors. *Above right:* One-armed Civil War Vet **General O O Howard**, who pursued Chief Joseph in the Nez Percé War, was a Christian warrior who sympathized with the Indians he fought.

Chief led his people in a long, roundabout and time-wasting detour. The delay gave Sturgis, now joined by Howard, the opportunity to catch up with him at Canyon Creek, near Billings, on 13 September 1877.

But Joseph held off Sturgis so successfully that the latter's critics, in their frustration, later accused him of timidity and even cowardice, although he lost three men killed and had 11 more wounded. The Nez Percés were tiring, but they slipped away from the battered Sturgis and headed for Bear Paw Mountain, only 40 miles from the safety of the Canadian border. On the northern slope, Joseph unwisely paused again to rest his exhausted people at the urging of Looking Glass.

Once more, their scouts failed the chiefs. Not all army units were behind them. The nemesis of the Sioux, Colonel Nelson Miles, had been alerted by couriers from Sturgis. Now he moved a strong unit to cut off the Nez Percé withdrawal. Miles had almost 400 men, mostly cavalry and infantrymen mounted on Indian ponies. He quickly moved northwestward, ferrying the Yellowstone and Missouri Rivers in a race with the Nez Percés for the Canadian line.

The Colonel's Sioux and Cheyenne scouts found the Nez Percé camp in the Bear Paw ravine of Snake Creek early on 30 September 1877. Miles attacked by mid-morning and found that, unaccountably, the Indians had again failed to post guards. The Nez Percés fled to the ridges, leaving teepees and ponies to the soldiers. Still, when units

of the 7th charged Indians on the heights above a cutbank, they were rebuffed with heavy losses. Like Modocs, the Nez Percés concentrated their fire on officers and non-commissioned officers. True, Miles had 22 enlisted men killed and 38 wounded, but a captain and a lieutenant were dead, two more captains and three lieutenants wounded. Seven sergeants were killed, including all three of the 7th's first sergeants. Three sergeants and a corporal were wounded. Such a casualty list was enough for Miles to give up his assault and to settle down to a siege.

The Nez Percés dug trenches with knives, tomahawks, even frying pans, as their sharpshooters dodged shells from the howitzer and the up-ended 'Napoleon' fieldpiece and exchanged fire with Miles's marksmen. Joseph sent a messenger to Sitting Bull, only a day distant, asking him to come to his aid. But the old chief did not come, or even answer the message.

Uncharacteristically, Miles seized Chief Joseph under a flag of truce, but had to release him in exchange for one of his lieutenants who strayed into the Nez Percé lines. General Howard arrived, but let Miles retain his command until he could accept the Nez Percé surrender.

Finally, after five days of siege, Chief Joseph decided that he had done all that he could for his surrounded people. He sent a message to Miles, asking him to tell Howard 'I am tired of fighting.' He then met with the two officers.

The Surrender of Chief Joseph

The handsome chief who rode into Miles's camp on 5 October wore buckskin leggings and, oddly, a gray woollen shawl—pierced with several bullet holes. His scalplock was tied with otter fur in part, the rest of it plaited in pigtails. His head and one wrist were slightly bloodied by bullet wounds. Ceremoniously, he gave his rifle to Miles, then smiled and shook Howard's hand. He surrendered 400 tribesmen, less than 100 of them warriors. About 100 of his men had joined Sitting Bull, along with 200 women and children.

Of his 800 people, Joseph lost 120 dead during his epic, three-month, 1700-mile retreat, more than half of them braves. The Nez Percés killed about 180 whites, mostly soldiers, and wounded about 150 more. They won some battles, accepted a draw or a defeat in one or two more, but consistently outmarched and outfought the Army. The whole country was impressed by the Nez Percés. Miles described them as 'the boldest men and best marksmen of any Indians I ever encountered.' Sherman praised them for their fighting skill and courage, but especially for their humanity. 'They abstained from scalping, let captive women go free, did not commit indiscriminate murder of peaceful families.'

Chief Joseph was not the only Nez Percé chief, of course. There was Looking Glass, and White Bird, also Toohool-hoolzote and the half-blood guide, Poker Joe. But it was Chief Joseph who most impressed the whites. Miles said of him that he was 'the highest type of Indian I have ever known; very handsome, brave, and kind . . . a man of more sagacity and intelligence than any Indian I have ever met. He counseled against the war and against the usual cruelties practiced by the Indians, and is far more humane than such Indians as Crazy Horse and Sitting Bull.'

Chief Joseph was one of the most eloquent of Indian orators. His moving words of surrender have been much quoted, by whites and Indians alike. 'I am tired of fighting. Our chiefs are killed. Looking Glass is dead . . . It is cold and we have no blankets. The little children are freezing to death . . .' The much-wronged Nez Percé closed his pathetic message—'I want to have time to look for my children and see how many of them I can find. Maybe I shall find them among the dead. Hear me, my chiefs, my heart is sick and sad. From where the sun now stands, I will fight no more, forever.'

After their heart-breaking ordeal, the Nez Percés were not allowed to go to Lapwai, as Miles had promised. He was overruled by Sheridan and Sherman. Over his protests, Joseph's people were exiled to distant Kansas and the Indian Territory. There, many sickened and died. Chief Joseph remained the tribe's leader. But even with the support of Generals Miles and Howard, he could not get the Government to return his people to the Northwest until 1885. His people were allowed to settle on Washington Territory's Colville Reservation, the followers of Looking Glass and White Bird on the Lapwai Reservation. But Oregonians refused to let Chief Joseph return to his beloved Wallowas, and he died at Colville in 1904.

As Howard, Gibbon and even Terry quarreled with the aggressive and arrogant Miles over the spoils of Nez Percé War glory, peace began to spread over the West. It was helped along by the Indian Bureau reforms of Interior Secretary Carl Schurz.

The Ute War

The Utes of Colorado, Kit Carson's old friends, were auxiliaries of the Army against Navajos and Plains Indians. Their main chief was a peaceful statesman, Ouray. Yet they went to war in 1879 after their country was overrun by silver-seeking whites.

The direct cause of the conflict was the utopianism of White River Indian Agent Nathan Meeker. He was determined to make instant farmers of the Utes. They resisted; he asked Army help. Major Thomas T Thornburgh was sent with a force of 153 men. Misunderstandings between him and the Ute leader, Jack, led to a fire-fight. Thornburgh was killed and his command, now under Captain J Scott Payne, badly mauled. He had lost ten dead and 42 wounded by the time a rescue party of black cavalrymen joined him, only to be pinned down also. Most of the horses and mules were dead, too. Escape was impossible, but Colonel Wesley Meritt, making one of his remarkable forced marches, broke the siege by driving the Utes away.

Ouray and Schurz tried to make peace but the Agency massacre and mistreatment of the women enraged the country. Army reinforcements poured into Colorado but Interior Department Special Agent Charles Adams released tensions and negotiated the release of the captives. The Ute War was ended by diplomacy. A commission decided that only a dozen Utes were guilty of the **Meeker Massacre**. They were tried for murder. The rest of the Utes were transferred to the Uintah Reservation in Utah.

The Bannocks

But peace was interrupted in a region supposedly pacified by Crook in the 1860s. The desert-ranging Bannocks and Western Shoshones of the Idaho-Oregon-Nevada border country became rebellious. Asked why, Crook answered, 'Hunger; nothing but hunger.'

But a stupid clerical error of 1868 helped bring about war a decade later. The clerk who was transcribing the terms of the treaty by mistake guaranteed a non-existent 'Kansas Prairie' to the Bannocks rather than their Camas

Above: The 1877 **Battle of Big Hole** was one of four Nez Percé War battles. Colonel John Gibbon took the village in only 20 minutes but the Nez Percés rallied, pinning the Army down in rifle pits until General Howard came to the rescue.

Prairie. Naturally, whites settled the latter. Several hundred of the Bannocks' kin, the Malheur Paiutes, joined them and when the Bannock chief, Buffalo Horn, was killed, the Paiute, Egan, succeeded him.

It was O O Howard's job to pacify the Bannocks and he did a better job than with the Nez Percés, thanks largely to Captain Reuben F Bernard. Winnemucca, chief of most of the Paiutes, did not want to fight and Bernard, through the chief's daughter, Sarah Winnemucca, arranged his defection and escape. Howard appointed the girl his interpreter.

It took Bernard just two skirmishes, plus one by Captain Evan Miles, to scatter the Bannocks, though the last did not surrender until September.

The Bannocks infected the tiny tribe of Sheepeaters, renegade Shoshones and Bannocks, with rebellion, too. These people lived by hunting mountain sheep in the rugged Salmon River Mountains of Idaho. They probably numbered about 50 fighting men in all, but their haunts were so inaccessible than even Bernard could not find them. They found Lieutenant Henry Catley, however, and ran him off so fast that he was courtmartialed. But dogged pursuit by small Army detachments wore them down and the 'mass' of the Sheepeater nation, 51 men, women and children, surrendered in October of 1878.

The Rise of Geronimo

Custer's disaster, and its aftermath, drew the public's attention away from the Mexican border. But it simmered in lawlessness and violence during the last half of the decade of the 1870s. However, General E O C Ord's raids from Texas into the former sanctuary of Mexico, actually carried out by Colonels Ranald Mackenzie and William Shafter and, especially by the black Seminole scouts of Lieutenant John Bullis, shifted frontier incursions westward into New Mexico and Arizona.

The two territories were ripe for trouble. Cochise, the peacemaker, had died in 1874 and Crook had been transferred away the following year. The best efforts of able Indian agents John P Clum and Tom Jeffords were frustrated by Apache truculence on the one hand and, on the other, by the Tucson Ring. This was a cabal of Army contractors and other sharp businessmen, politicians, whiskey peddlers and gun runners.

Concentrating different bands of Apaches on the San Carlos reservation was a monumental, disastrous, bureaucratic error. It ensured the rise of cruel and cunning Geronimo as leader of the Chiricahuas who refused to go to the agency. Clum bravely arrested him and dragged him and his people to San Carlos, but the Warm Springs chief, Victorio, led a mass exodus of both bands in 1877.

The Apaches marauded more into Mexico than in the American Southwest, which did not particularly disturb the US Army. But there were enough atrocities north of the line for cavalry companies, joined by cowboy volunteers and Texas Rangers, to chase Victorio's Warm Springs Chiricahuas and Mescaleros through Arizona, New Mexico, Texas and Mexico in 1877–79.

Victorio ambushed two Mexican parties in 1879 and slipped out of a trap set for him by Colonel Edward Hatch

Right: Charles Russell documented the awe of the Plains Indians who spied the first **fireboats** ascending the Missouri River.

in April 1880. It was almost impossible to run him down, though he was bested—and wounded—by a company of Indian Army scouts in May of 1880. He would stop to fight only when he could choose the ground. He and his followers rode their horses to death, then ate them and stole new mounts. Cavalry horses became so utterly exhausted that it can be said that Victorio dismounted the 9th Regiment. Colonel Hatch complained of Victorio's secret ally—the terrain. Compared to the San Mateo Mountains or the Black Range, he said, the Modoc Lava Beds country was a lawn!

When Victorio switched his border raiding back to the east again, he ran afoul of an almost-forgotten Civil War hero, Colonel Benjamin Grierson of Grierson's Raid. The Colonel surfaced from obscurity quickly by posting his tough black cavalrymen as guards on the critically-few desert waterholes. Twice in July and August 1880 he turned Victorio back, at Tinaja de las Palmas in Quitman Canyon, and again at Rattlesnake Spring, and forced him to retire into Mexico.

At last, in 1880, diplomacy—and common sense—triumphed over suspicion and nationalistic jealousies. Mexico and the United States cooperated against their common menace, Apache raiders. They encircled Victorio in the Tres Castillos Mountains of Mexico. There, Colonel Joaquín Terrazas sent the Americans home, however, ostensibly because he did not trust the Apache scouts of Captain George Buell. Probably he just did not want to share any glory with them. Terrazas trapped and killed Victorio on 15 October 1880, along with 60 of his fighting men and about 18 women and children.

The old chief, Nana, succeeded Victorio, although he was 70, rheumatic, and had only about 15 warrior-followers. He led the Army on another exhausting chase through New Mexico in the summer of 1881, fighting in more than a half-dozen skirmishes and murdering ranchers and miners before heading westward into Arizona and Sonora to join Geronimo as his lieutenant.

The Apache Wars

There were many chiefs still active in Arizona during the 1880s, including Nana, Chato, and Nachez, Cochise's son,

but it was a merciless non-chief, Geronimo, who took over the leadership of Apache resistance to the increasing white settlement of the territory.

Boredom, liquor (*tizwin*) and the natural inter-band antipathies made the restless San Carlos Reservation into a training ground for 'renegades,' warlike Warm Springs and Chiricahua Apaches. Crook termed them the 'tigers of the human race.' If they needed an excuse to strike out on the war trail again, it came in 1881.

Not only the White Mountain Apaches but even some of the Army's own Apache Scouts at that time fell under the spell of a shaman who anticipated the Ghost Dance.

Nakaidoklini claimed to have the proper medicine to raise dead warriors to life and to rid Arizona of its troublesome whites.

Indian Bureau pressure brought Colonel Eugene Carr on the run. Nakaidoklini submitted to arrest but, that evening, his followers attacked Carr at Cibicú Creek. It was 30 August. At the same time, Carr's White Mountain Scouts mutinied. They shot Captain Edmund Hentig in the back, killing him, then killed six soldiers and wounded two more. The shaman tried to escape by crawling off into the brush but Sergeant John MacDonald, though wounded in one leg, shot him three times in the head. (Some say that he

Below: During the **Apache campaign** against Geronimo in 1885, men of A Troop, 6th US Cavalry, took a coffee break around shady trees of the desert mountains of the Arizona-Mexico border.

Below: Frederick Remington was Charles Russell's major rival as the foremost artist depicting the nineteenth century West. Both men were accurate interpreters of Indians, and of cowboys as well, but Remington excelled in his pictures of Army life. His camp scene was painted late in the Indian Wars; **the cavalry troopers wore new web belts** for their 45/70 Springfield carbines.

FREDERIC REMINGTON-

Bottom: Camillus S Fly happened on **two Apache men at their family ranchería** with all the comforts of home – *olla* and basket, remains of a cookfire, brush *wickiups*, and trusty Springfield rifles. *Below:* **Peaches**, looking delicate and timid for an Apache Scout who favored the gunman's cross-draw, posed for Ben Wittick in the natural surroundings of a studio's prop yuccas and junipers.

survived the gunshots and had to be finished off with an axe.)

The shaman's converts and the treacherous scouts got Carr's horses, but the colonel led a night withdrawal which probably saved Fort Apache. Rarely, indeed, did Indians ever try an assault on a garrisoned post but, after cutting the telegraph wires, the Apaches surrounded and attacked Fort Apache, and actually overran some of the post's outbuildings before they were driven off.

Reinforcements rushed in and most of the culprits surrendered. Some of the mutinous Apache Scouts were hanged and some were imprisoned on Alcatraz Island in San Francisco Bay. Carr was accused of incompetence by his superior, General Orlando B Willcox, but a court of inquiry largely vindicated him. His major error—surely a human one—was in trusting his heretofore loyal Apache Scouts too much.

While Army officers wrangled over responsibility for the Cibicú fight and mutiny, the Chiricahuas decamped from the reservation and ran for Mexico. From there, Geronimo, Nachez, Chato and Juh were soon raiding the Gila Valley, killing between 30 and 50 whites in April of 1882. Lieutenant Colonel George A Forsyth soon engaged the enemy in a desperate fight, but they got away and turned back another unit which followed them into Mexico. Forsyth then chased them even deeper into that country, stopping only when ordered out by a colonel of Mexican infantry who had just ambushed the fleeing, unwary Apaches. At a cost of 22 dead and 16 wounded, his men killed 78 Indians and captured 33 more. But most of them were women or children, not fighters.

In July 1882 White Mountain 'renegades' took to the field and tried to trap Captain Adna Chaffee's troop on the Mogollón Rim's Crook Trail between Camp Verde and Fort Apache. But scout Al Sieber discovered the trap and Chaffee attacked the ambushers. He enjoyed that rare

luxury, a conventional pitched battle with his opponents, and thrashed them. He killed 20-odd warriors and probably wounded all the rest before they fled the scene. The Army misnamed the fight, calling it the **Battle of Big Dry Wash** when it actually took place at East Clark Creek.

Sherman now replaced the controversial Willcox by recalling Crook, who took over on 4 September 1882 and set about correcting a sorry situation. He saw three tasks as being necessary: to re-establish control over the reservation Indians; to crush hostiles operating from Mexico's Sierra Madre and, the result of these two measures, to protect the lives and properties of Arizona's citizens.

Crook personally visited the reservations with only a small escort. He threw squatters off Indian land. He put together a cadre of officers who knew the Apaches, like Captain Emmet Crawford and Lieutenant Charles Gatewood. They recruited trustworthy Apache Scouts who patrolled the border.

Not until 1883 were the so-called renegades able to mount a raid into Arizona again. But Chato looted and murdered his way from the Fort Huachuca area to New Mexico and back to Chihuahua, making fools of the military and volunteers who tried to chase and intercept him.

Skirmishes in Mexico

A furious Sherman ordered Crook to destroy the Apache hostiles and to ignore the international boundary. Crook took the precaution of conferring with the authorities in Sonora and Chihuahua first, then penetrated the rugged Sierra Madre. His force was a small efficient one—almost 200 Apache Scouts under Crawford and Gatewood, plus Chaffee's 45 6th Cavalry troopers. They were supported by 350 pack mules and guided by a crack Apache 'friendly' nicknamed Peaches by his Army buddies.

Crook's patience, thoroughness and doggedness paid off.

Crawford stormed and destroyed an Apache village on 15 May. Crook was able to persuade all of the chiefs but Juh to give up Chato, Benito, Loco, Nachez, Nana and even Geronimo came in, though the last-named was laggardly and appeared to be reneging on his agreement to surrender. He did not join the others on the San Carlos Reservation until March of 1884.

By a tenacious pusuit rather than rounding up his enemy, Crook won his Sierra Madre campaign of 1883 in spectacular fashion, silencing his jeering critics and proving his theories of Indian-style warfare. He kept a watchful eye on his charges at San Carlos, now completely under Army, not Indian Bureau, control. He used Apache spies as intelligence agents and when young Kaytennae challenged his authority, sent the Apache to Alcatraz prison.

But, after a big *tizwin* binge, all of the chiefs except Chato bolted for Mexico, some of them raiding while en route. Crook, from his new headquarters, Fort Bowie in Apache Pass, first locked up the border with 3000 soldiers, mostly cavalry, patrolling and guarding every watering place between the Santa Cruz River, south of Tucson, to the Rio Grande. Behind them he placed a second line of defense, a reserve force scattered along the Southern Pacific track. Then he sent Crawford and Lieutenant Wirt Davis deep into Mexico with mixed units of cavalry and scouts. (The reciprocal border-crossing agreement with Mexico had been renewed.)

Four times in the summer of 1885 the punitive parties hit the Apaches but, each time, they evaporated from view in the hot desert air, their losses very small. Two bands even counterattacked, one giving Crook's heavy border patrols the slip and stealing horses in southeast Arizona Territory. Worse, a little-known warrior, Josanie, led a month-long

Below: In 1883 a 6th Cavalry unit en route to Fort Apache, Arizona, from Mexico, made camp just outside of Zuñi Pueblo, New Mexico.

Below: Charles Russell's 1908 painting, **The Medicine Man**, portrayed a shaman taking the lead in breaking up and moving a village by travois to a new location near the shallow ruts of the Overland Trail on the open grasslands of the High Plains country.

Top: **Geronimo and his Chiracahua Apaches** lined up ominously on a grassy ridge dotted with clumps of Spanish bayonet, or yucca.
Above: **Geronimo** in March 1886.

raid with another war party that covered 1200 miles of both territories. He killed almost 40 people without an Army patrol even sighting him, much less cutting him off.

By now, Crook so trusted his Apache Scouts that he sometimes sent them, without any regulars along, to track and fight their own kin. In January of 1886, Crawford hit the enemy again and secured a truce for a parley. But Mexican militiamen attacked Geronimo's camp. When Crawford tried to stop the shooting, the Mexicans shot him dead. Still, Geronimo and other chiefs talked with his lieutenant and agreed to meet Crook in two months.

Crook demanded unconditional surrender at a meeting, 25–27 March, a dozen miles below the border. He swore, 'If you stay out, I'll keep after you and kill the last one [of you], if it takes 50 years.' Shortly however, he relented and offered terms. He then wired news of Geronimo's surrender to Sheridan—too soon. Nana and Geronimo got drunk on *tizwin* again and fled to the mountains.

Sheridan, who distrusted Crook's Apache Scouts, was angry at him for letting Geronimo slip through his fingers. Now he demanded unconditional surrender or the complete destruction of the Apaches—including those who had already surrendered to Crook on his terms. Crook's honor was at stake. On 1 April 1886 he asked to be relieved of his command. Sheridan hurriedly replaced him with Miles.

Sheridan ordered Miles to depend on his regulars, not Indian scouts. He did so. He also added heliograph stations to the telegraph lines to improve communications between mobile columns. But he sent Captain Henry Lawton into Mexico in May to harass and wear out the Apaches, with Apache Scouts as guides. At the same time, his defensive forces chased a raiding party out of the Santa Cruz Valley and back into Mexico.

Lawton's march was a grueling one, mostly on foot, as the horses gave out in the desert sun during the first week. The Captain lost 40 pounds of weight and his surgeon, Dr Leonard Wood, lost 30. Enlisted men had to be replaced with new rankers as they wilted and dropped during the 2000-mile march. Only once did Lawton catch up with the Apaches, on 14 July, and they got away, unscathed.

In the meantime, Miles made sure that there would be no reinforcements for the hostiles from the San Carlos

Reservation. He rounded up the agency's Chiricahuas and exiled them to Fort Marion, Florida, by train. Then he persuaded the brave Gatewood, though ill, to risk his life by 'talking in' Geronimo as Crawford had almost done. He was the only officer left in the Department of Arizona who had Geronimo's trust.

The Surrender of Geronimo

Geronimo finally agreed to give up, but only to Miles. The General took his surrender at Skeleton Canyon, 65

Below: **General George Crook** was the Army's least-by-the-book soldier. He bested the Apaches of Arizona and New Mexico in developing a style of warfare to counter their hit-and-run guerrilla tactics. He used Apache Scouts like Dutchy (left) and Alchiso (Alchisay) skilfully against their hostile kin. He preferred mules, like his faithful *Apache*, over horses because they withstood the heat and fatigue of Southwest desert campaigning better than any breed of horse.

miles south of Apache Pass, on 4 September 1886, after Miles guaranteed that the renegades' lives would be spared and that they would not be separated from their families. The prisoners entrained for Florida.

Left: **Apache prisoners,** Fort Bowie, Arizona, 1884.

Below left: The National Anthropological Archives, Smithsonian Institution, has a rich collection of photos like this view of the **Arapaho Ghost Dance,** c. 1893, by James Mooney of the Bureau of American Ethnology.

Overleaf: J McDonald in 1886 photographed **Geronimo** (first row. third from right) and **Chiricahua prisoners** as the Apaches rested on an Arizona railroad embankment below well-guarded passenger coaches that would carry them off into exile in Florida. By 1894, however, Geronimo was back in the West at Fort Sill, Oklahoma.

Now President Cleveland ordered that the Apaches be held at Fort Bowie for criminal trials. But when Miles protested, like Crook, that he had given his word, the President came around on this point of Army honor. However, the men were separated from their families in Florida. In any case, they all sickened and died equally in the humid climate, including the loyal Apache Scouts. Crook now joined the Indian Rights Association to seek justice for his old enemies. To his discredit, Miles did not.

Crook died in 1890 but, four years later, the dwindling Apache survivors were allowed to migrate to Fort Sill, Oklahoma, over Miles's opposition. (There Geronimo died in 1909.) In 1913 some were allowed to move to New Mexico's Mescalero Reservation.

Partisans of Crook and Miles squared off to claim credit for the termination of the Apache Wars. The pro-Crook war correspondent, Charles Lummis, wrote of 'the mongrel pack which has barked at the heels of this patient commander.' The careers of the former's protéges, Lawton and Wood, advanced, but Crook's brave subordinate, Gatewood, was forgotten. He died, only a first lieutenant, in 1896.

The self-centered Miles closed out the Apache Wars because he was an excellent officer. But students of these bloody and difficult campaigns realize that he could do so only because of the groundwork done by Crook. And it is his predecessor, Crook, who remains the real Army hero of the Apache Wars.

The Ghost Dance and the Death of Sitting Bull

All apparent Indian resistance in the West crumbled with Geronimo's surrender. The Army's only four-star general made it official in a retirement letter of 1883. 'I now regard the Indians as substantially eliminated from the problems of the Army . . .' But Sherman was realist enough to warn of the possibility of temporary, spasmodic Indian alarms.

Just such a delayed—almost post-mortem—spasm occurred in 1890. It was touched off, ironically, by a peace-mongering Paiute mystic. Nevada's Wovoka was a half-Christianized seer, last in a long line of Indian messiahs—Popé, Pontiac, The Prophet, Smohalla, Nakaidoklini and Sword Bearer. His religion was called the Ghost Dance because he taught that praying, singing and, particularly, dancing would give the Indians a look at a joyous new world in which the dead would rise up to greet their living friends.

Many tribes adopted the Ghost Dance religion, but the Teton Sioux, Kicking Bear and Short Bull, interpreted Wovoka's prophecies to mean the destruction of the whites as a necessary preparation for the new world. They ignored his appeals to non-violence and talked instead of the medicine of ghost shirts which would turn away the white man's bullets.

General Miles was not as sanguine as Sherman about the end of Indian troubles and was ready when the Ghost Dance fervor boiled over on the Pine Ridge and Rosebud reservations in 1890. There, the Oglala and Brulé Sioux danced themselves into exhausted but euphoric stupors in which they dreamed of an American Indian holy war. Miles responded promptly by having the Army occupy both agencies and split apart the Ghost Dance's potential hostiles from Sioux friendlies.

The 600 followers of Wovoka, of both bands, then joined together in the Stronghold on the edge of the Pine Ridge Reservation. The major Sioux chiefs who were attracted by the cult were Hump, Big Foot and Sitting Bull. Hump was pacified or neutralized, but Miles ordered the arrest of the other two men. The Standing Rock Reservation's agent, James McLaughlin, urged that Sitting Bull be apprehended by his own people. The local Army Commandant agreed.

At dawn of 15 December 1890 Lieutenant Bull Head and 40-odd uniformed Indian Police surrounded Sitting Bull's cabin. Meek when he was at first detained, he called for help outside when he saw about 160 cultists watching the arrest take place. An old enemy of Bull Head, Catch the Bear, shot the Lieutenant dead. But before he fell, Bull Head put a ball in Sitting Bull's body and Officer Red Tomahawk added a pistol bullet to his head. The police then stood their ground in a shoot-out until they were reinforced by a squadron of the 8th Cavalry. Six Indian policemen were dead or dying, and an equal number of Ghost Dancers, including Sitting Bull.

Miles moved more troops in to contain the cult. But, to his surprise, there was little or no violence after Sitting Bull's death. True, bands slipped away from the reservations to the Badlands. But Hump, for example, got most of his 400 Hunkpapas to halt their flight and surrender.

The largest band of presumed hostiles was that of old Big Foot, Miniconjous and 40 or so Hunkpapas. Miles ordered Colonel Edmund V Sumner to round up the chief, but the veteran officer stalled. He argued that an arrest was unnecessary and counter-productive, probably inciting a fight.

The Battle of Wounded Knee

Big Foot, frightened by the Army's warlike preparations, fled with his people toward the Pine Ridge Agency. Miles, assuming that he was heading for the Stronghold and the irreconcilables, was angry at Sumner for letting him get away. He sent several units to intercept him and prevent him rendezvousing with the Brulés and Oglalas. One of these forces was the 7th Cavalry, Custer's old outfit.

Big Foot consented to being escorted to Pine Ridge by the military. But Colonel James W Forsyth (not to be confused with the hero of Beecher's Island, George Forsyth) had orders from Miles both to disarm Big Foot's people and to march them to the railroad for shipment to Omaha. All this was, of course, against Sumner's advice.

When the Sioux encampment awakened on the morning of 29 December 1890, its people found that Forsyth had surrounded them with 500 troops and had posted four rapid-firing Hotchkiss cannon to cover them.

As the squaws began to break camp and pack up to move, Forsyth lined up the 120 men and ordered them to turn in

Indian Reservations 1880

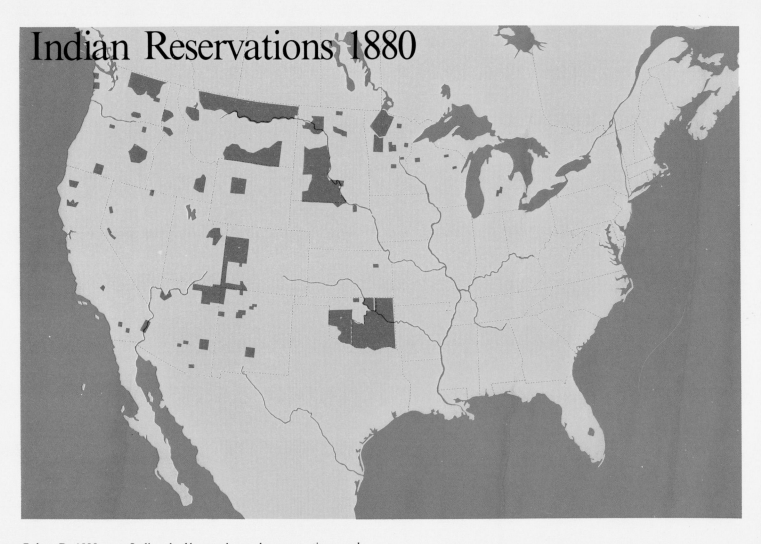

Below: By 1890, most Indians had been relocated to reservations, such as the **Sioux Reservation** seen here.

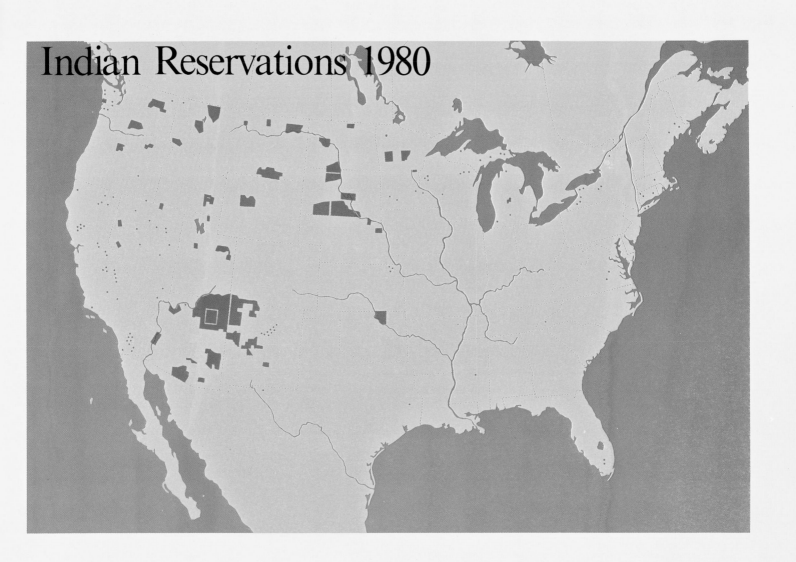

Indian Reservations 1980

Below: A mass grave was dug for the Sioux dead at **Wounded Knee**. Some 150 Sioux were buried.

Above: In 1891 **Army officers of the Battle of Wounded Knee** – who should have hung their heads in shame – posed proudly for the camera.

their weapons. When only a few token guns, mostly broken, were surrendered, he searched the lodges and found arms and ammunition hidden in them. Next, he ordered a body search of the Sioux, men and women, for weapons concealed under their blankets.

The Sioux were angered by this humiliating procedure, of course, and a young shaman, Yellow Bird, began reminding the warriors of their protective ghost shirts. A few braves threw off their blankets to reveal carbines and rifles. A single soldier and a warrior got into a scuffle. Someone, probably this enlisted man, fired a shot, perhaps accident-

ally. (The Army blamed an anonymous enlisted scapegoat— a curious kind of Unknown Soldier for the service to single out.)

Forsyth's troops opened fire on the crowded camp at close range. The soldiers were excited, scared, perhaps vengeful, remembering Little Bighorn. Their small arms fire was deadly at such close quarters, but it paled before the bloody work of the Hotchkiss guns.

To the Indians and many sympathetic whites, the **Battle of Wounded Knee** was no battle at all, but a massacre. That it was, but only in part. It was not a massacre in the sense of the deliberate slaughter of Sand Creek in 1864. For it was also a battle or, at least, a real skirmish. Forsyth lost 25 officers and men killed, and had 39 wounded. Big Foot and his medicine man, Yellow Bird, were among the 150 Sioux dead on the frozen ground. There were another 50 Indians wounded. Probably the large number of women and children, 62, among the Sioux casualties was the result of wild firing by riflemen and Hotchkiss gunners at close quarters. In fact, some of the Army's own dead and wounded were the accidental result of gunshot and shrapnel wounds from friendly fire.

The public was horrified by Wounded Knee and compared it to Sand Creek. Miles saw it as a stupendous blunder by Forsyth. He relieved him of his command and summoned a court of inquiry. The testimony seemed to show that his soldiers tried to avoid shooting non-combatants, but that this was impossible. Miles found Forsyth to be guilty of incompetence and irresponsible disobedience of orders. The Secretary of War and General John M Schofield reversed his decision, however, and restored Forsyth to duty.

As if to prove that Miles was right, Forsyth blundered into a trap set by the Sioux at Drexel Mission. While pinned down, the victor of Wounded Knee lost one officer and

Below: W R Cross of Hot Springs, S D, photographed the **rifled guns, field artillery,** on the Pine Ridge Reservation in 1891.

Below: **Lieutenant Taylor** and **Indian scouts** at Pine Ridge, 1891.

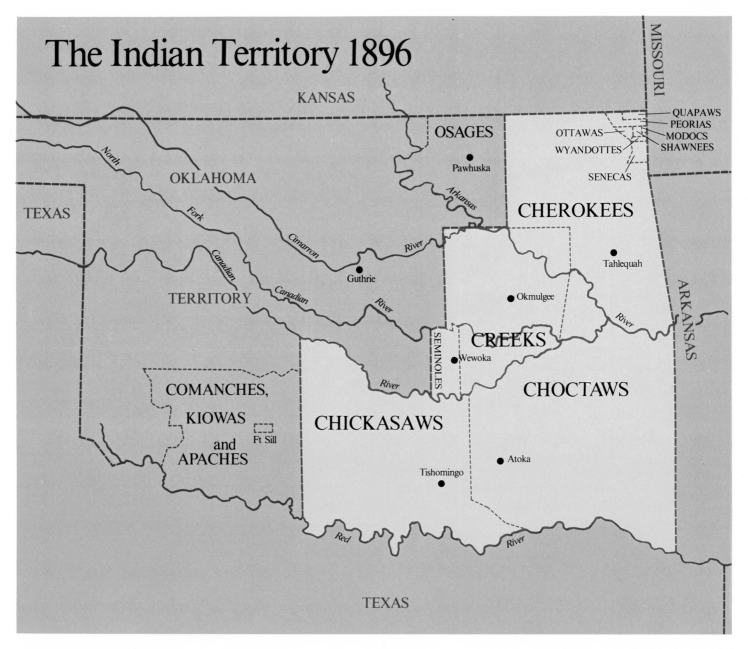

The Indian Territory 1896

Above: The government established **Indian Territory** in the land west of Arkansas for the five Civilized Tribes in 1830. **Indian Territory** merged with Oklahoma and ceased to exist in 1907 when Oklahoma joined the Union.

one enlisted man, dead, and had five more wounded. He lost more face when he had to be rescued by the 9th Cavalry.

But Miles had erred, too, in ordering Forsyth to disarm the Sioux and entrain them to Omaha. As Sumner said, Big Foot could have been escorted peacefully, to Pine Ridge had the Colonel not tried to seize all Indian weapons.

Miles was more careful now. He employed a judicious mix of diplomacy and force to surround the remaining 'hostiles.' Unlike Forsyth, he left some breathing room between the two forces. And while he kept at a respectful distance, he began to tighten the circle around the Sioux at the same time that he sent Indian peace emissaries among them. They soon gave up. Kicking Bird, last to surrender, gave his Winchester to Miles on 15 January 1891.

Wounded Knee, by sheer coincidence, occurred in the year in which statisticians of the Census Bureau declared there was no longer a line of frontier settlement in the West.

The Army was only the cutting edge of so-called civilization. It was the power behind it, the Industrial Revolution, that conquered the Indians with its railroads, barbed wire,

telegraph, six-shooters, howitzers. And the Industrial Revolution's agents were not only soldiers but farmers, ranchers, miners, townsfolk and the buffalo hunters who utterly destroyed the Plains Indians' life-support system in one short decade.

In a sense, the Army was left with the dirty work by others. It was called in at the last moment, usually, to clean up a mess made by civilians. The old Sioux spokesman was thinking of ordinary citizens, not troopers, when he sagely observed of the whites, 'They made us many promises, more than I can remember, but they never kept but one; they promised to take our land, and they took it.'

The melting pot theory of assimilation had not worked in the face of the long conflict of cultures, the clashing of races, on the plains, mountains and deserts of the West any better than in the hardwood forests and meadows of the East. So war, in place of peace, became the sorry 'solution' to what was euphemized by politicians as the nation's 'Indian problem.' After a thousand bloody actions, in which the Army had 2000 casualties and the Indians three times that number, Teddy Roosevelt's winning of the West finally came to pass. But at tremendous cost, not only for the losers, the Indians, but also for the winners.

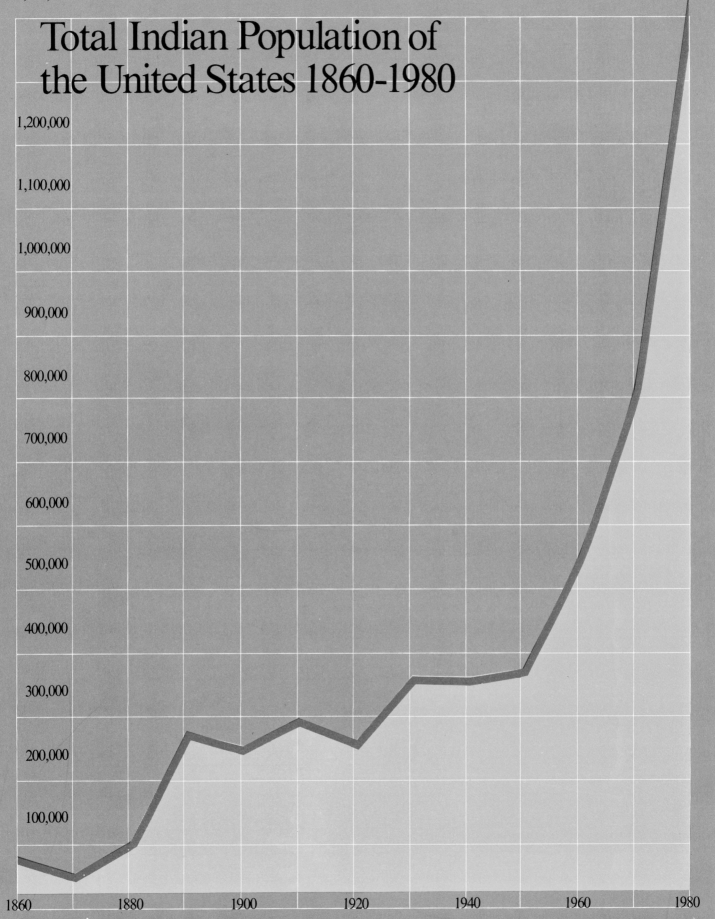

Total Indian Population of the United States 1860-1980

1,400,000

1,200,000

1,100,000

1,000,000

900,000

800,000

700,000

600,000

500,000

400,000

300,000

200,000

100,000

1860   1880   1900   1920   1940   1960   1980

Note: The 1860 US Census was the first in which the Indian Population was counted as a separate group. Estimates for the years prior to 1860 vary widely but are generally accepted to have been higher than the 1860 level. They probably averaged, for the preceding century, somewhere between the 1880 and 1890 levels.

Below: A Plains Indian horse *travois*. This means of transport survived even after the Indians made the transition from a nomadic to a reservation lifestyle.

Indian Population by State 1890

(Twenty most populous states.) Total = 249,273*

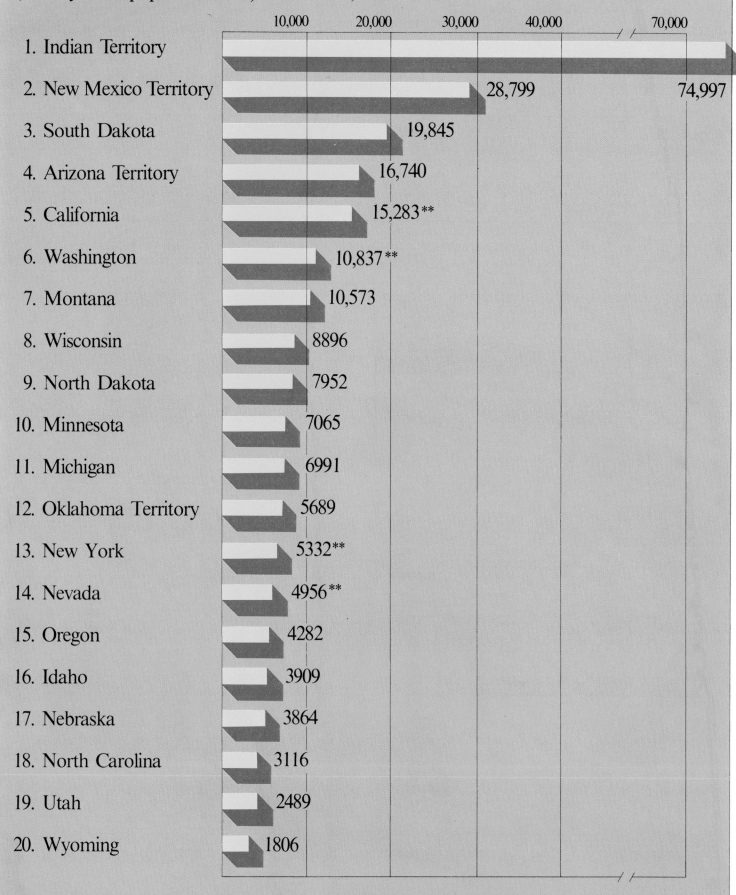

	10,000	20,000	30,000	40,000	70,000
1. Indian Territory					74,997
2. New Mexico Territory		28,799			
3. South Dakota	19,845				
4. Arizona Territory	16,740				
5. California	15,283**				
6. Washington	10,837**				
7. Montana	10,573				
8. Wisconsin	8896				
9. North Dakota	7952				
10. Minnesota	7065				
11. Michigan	6991				
12. Oklahoma Territory	5689				
13. New York	5332**				
14. Nevada	4956**				
15. Oregon	4282				
16. Idaho	3909				
17. Nebraska	3864				
18. North Carolina	3116				
19. Utah	2489				
20. Wyoming	1806				

*This figure includes 568 Indians listed as War Department prisoners.

**In all of the states listed, much less than a quarter of the Indian population lived off the reservations, with the exception of Washington, where 27% lived off-reservation, California (67%), Nevada (69%) and New York (100%).

Indian Population by State 1980

(Twenty most populous states.)   Total = 1,418,195

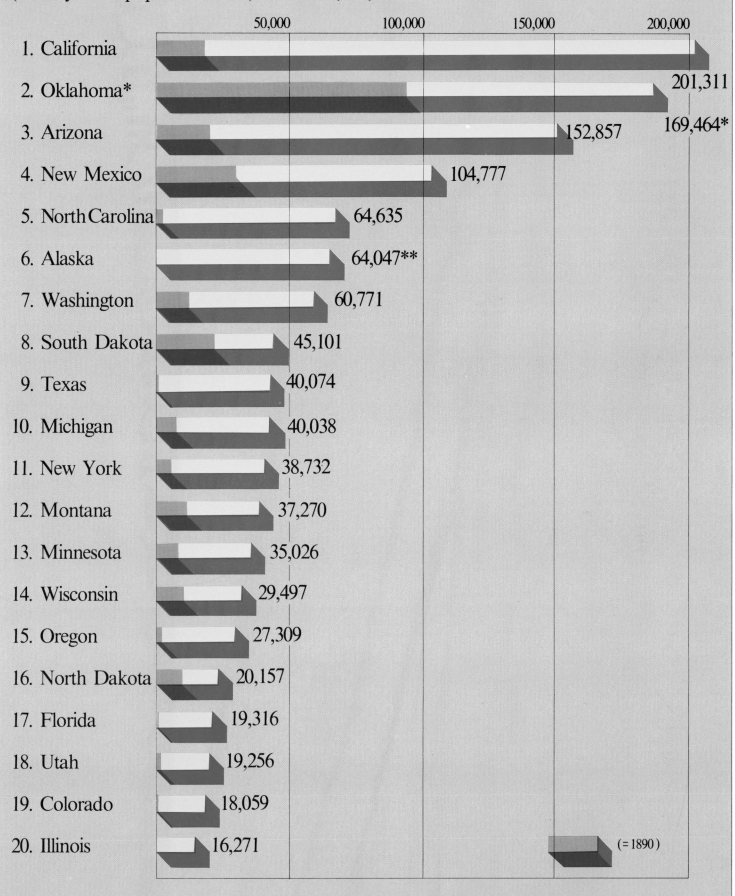

	50,000	100,000	150,000	200,000
1. California				
2. Oklahoma*				201,311
3. Arizona			152,857	169,464*
4. New Mexico		104,777		
5. North Carolina	64,635			
6. Alaska	64,047**			
7. Washington	60,771			
8. South Dakota	45,101			
9. Texas	40,074			
10. Michigan	40,038			
11. New York	38,732			
12. Montana	37,270			
13. Minnesota	35,026			
14. Wisconsin	29,497			
15. Oregon	27,309			
16. North Dakota	20,157			
17. Florida	19,316			
18. Utah	19,256			
19. Colorado	18,059			
20. Illinois	16,271			(= 1890)

*The State of Oklahoma, created in 1907, constituted a merger of the former Oklahoma Territory and Indian Territory.

**The Indian Population of Alaska was not counted in 1890.

Index

Page references in italics refer to illustrations.

Picture Credits

Below: Between 1867-74 Will Soule of Fort Sill, Oklahoma, took a picture of the lodge of a chief, **Little Big Mouth**, perhaps a Cheyenne, to show details of construction. It was made of buffalo hide (hair-side inside) sewed with thongs on travois poles, its doorway closed by a flap held in place by wooden pegs. At its apex the conical tent was ventilated by a hole with smoke flaps that could be shifted according to the wind.